Activating

Her

Eagle Instincts

A Unique 21-Day Devotional Digest

Hilette A. Virgo

M000031442

Activating Her Eagle Instincts | A Unique 21-Day Devotional Digest. Copyright © 2019. Hilette A. Virgo.

All rights reserved. No portion of this book may be reproduced, stored in a retrieval system, or transmitted in any form or by any means – electronic, mechanical, photocopy, recording, scanning, or other – except for a brief quotation in critical reviews or articles, without the prior written permission of the publisher or author.

Published by:

ISBN: 9781099601866 (paperback)

Unless otherwise stated, Scripture quotations marked KJV are from the Holy Bible, King James Version (Authorized Version). First published in 1611. Quoted from the KJV Classic Reference Bible, Copyright 1983, by The Zondervan Corporation.

Dedicated to my mom, Sonia, who is as wise, determined, fierce, protective, principled, regal, astute, classic and strong as an eagle.

Table of Contents

Acknowledgement

This dream materialized only because someone had invested in me; someone cheered, inspired, coached, supported, believed in and prayed for me. God sent me the best destiny helpers. God did it!

My dad, Henry Virgo, is simply the best. I credit my insatiable appetite for the Word of God to him. He stimulated my palate and fed me with delectable dishes and nuggets of Scriptures from a tender age. God blessed me immensely when He chose you to be my dad. I salute you my preacher and spiritual teacher.

To Joan Thaxter Randall, my coach: Crystal Daye, and cheerleaders, God positioned you in my life to be the midwives of my dream. You made the delivery most bearable with your soothing words of encouragement and direction.

To Omar and Natalya Phinn, my brother and sister in righteousness, God used you to usher me through one of the darkest times in my life. The devotions we had in your personal sanctuary stimulated and inspired me to find my wings. I appreciate you.

To Rowan Foster and Austin Sawe, my spiritual brothers and supporters, you were my crutches on days when I thought I would lose it. You offered technical support and encouraged me on this project. You are appreciated.

To Nadian Reid, Deneise Fearon and Tasharae Nicholson, my coach sisters, your words of encouragement, prayers and cheers warmed my heart and kept me afloat throughout this project.

To Mom, the superhero in my life, I am at a loss for words to express my appreciation for you. You held it down throughout. You have always supported my dreams and have been my pillar of strength. Thank you for your patience and the high standard you established. You are my Queen Eagle.

Foreword

Inspiring, thought-provoking, riveting, brilliant and relatable are few of the words that best captures the experience of the reader as she goes along the journey of *"Activating Her Eagle Instincts."* This book is most powerful in recognition and reconciliation of subtle yet profound metaphors to help its readers unlock their full potential. It encourages readers to embrace who they are and who they were created to be as they fulfill their God-given purpose.

The challenges of womanhood - rife with feelings of being odd, strange, intimidating and outspoken are brilliantly wrapped in the sheets of affirmation and encouragement. Nia's journey is our journey! Her story is our story! It is relatable to the young, driven, talented specimen of a woman who is charting her own course as she yearns to defy all odds and *"activate"* her full potential. It challenges her to be more loyal to her purpose than the voices of her critics. It challenges the reader to view failure as a learning experience and to rebound from such an experience stronger, wiser and better prepared to walk into her God-given destiny.

Chauna-Kaye Pottinger Ms. PMP
Christian, Wife, Mother, Blogger, Project Management Practitioner

Prologue

Once there was a hunter who found a huge and interesting nest on one of his hunting exploits along a mountain trail. The nest had a huge, plain egg inside, which somehow fascinated him. The adventurous boy in him couldn't resist and so, without giving it much thought, he reached in, extracted the egg and brought it home as a gift to his beautiful wife.

When the wife saw the egg that her husband took home, she looked at it closely and realized that a baby bird was developing inside and was almost ready to hatch. Instinctively, she brought it to a small chicken coop they had out in a barn at the back and placed it in a nest where a mother hen was incubating her eggs.

Within days, all ten eggs hatched, including the large, unique one that the hunter's wife had placed in the hen's nest. Among the brood of soft, yellow, fuzzy chicks was a brown, gangly, awkward looking overgrown baby chicken. But mother hen didn't seem to be bothered by this strange looking hatchling. In fact, she took care of it as if it was her own and named her Nia.

Nia had different features from her siblings and as they grew, she realized she was much bigger than all of them. She also had a different personality type that seemed to clash with theirs.

Because she was larger physically and was a lot more agile, she won all the games they played. No one wanted to play with her after a while though, because she was always winning.

Nia had a keen vision and would always see the worms and bugs before all her brothers and sisters. She was very kind and always shared her pickings, but her siblings did not appreciate this as they envied her for her hunting skills.

Despite her size and strength, she was very gentle with her family. But she would get extremely fierce when a stray or any other menacing animal threatened any of her siblings or relatives. This protective instinct was gravely resented by the chicken brood as it made her stand out as the hero among them. They would often encircle her angrily after such an episode and accuse her of trying to make them all look bad. No form of reasoning would cause them to see that she had just saved them. They failed to see that her actions were sincere and if she hadn't intervened when she did, they would not have the privilege of swinging verbal assaults at her in the aftermath of the combat.

Nia was sharp and quick-witted and outshone them in everything they did, and this made them distance themselves from her and speak about her every chance they got. It didn't matter to them that she could hear the snarls, sneers and scowls hurled at her character. This made her feel guilty for always having the right answer and, as a result, she held back many times just so she didn't offend her siblings.

The one thing they out-mastered her in was, ironically, what they despised her the most for, and that was bickering and being petty. Nia never got involved in their quarrels or took a side when they had their regular squabbles and they took grave offence to this. She always walked away when a quarrel started and left them to wrangle about whatever issues they had.

No matter how they sought an audience with her to discuss their other brothers or sisters, she just wouldn't entertain any form of gossip or tattle-tailing from any of them. This made them especially mad as they interpreted her disinterest as acting as if she was better than them. As she grew older, they ostracized her more and more.

When they all came of age and were fully mature, all her chicken siblings found themselves a mate. Not one of the chickens in the coop or the barn yard found her attractive or approached her to be their companion. She had no friends, and no one seemed to bother with her. She thought they all hated and scorned her. Little did she know that they all had a mixture of fear, envy, jealousy and loads of respect for her. But they just couldn't understand why she had to be so superior, gifted, strong, agile, beautiful and different. Her presence intimidated them and highlighted their inadequacy. They all wished they were her.

Nia, on the other hand, felt sad, lonely and useless. She spent her days in a corner of the barn wishing she was like the rest of her siblings: smaller, slower, weaker, not so smart and a little pettier. Why couldn't she be normal? Why couldn't she find their jokes as funny as they did? Why couldn't she squabble all day long and pick fights as they did? Why wasn't she enjoying just strolling around the barn and eating worms, bugs, corn and the grains the hunter's wife fed them? Why did she look and sound so different from them?

She really wanted to just hang her head and cry, but she couldn't. She wasn't even capable of whining and throwing tantrums and clucking like her family. Every time she tried to hang her head like her counterparts when she became sad, she unconsciously lifted it instead and looked to the sky. What was in the sky that was beckoning to her so much and caused her to be constantly gazing beyond the clouds? It would appear as if she was anticipating something or someone great to rescue her.

Then, one fateful day, as she looked up after a torturous session of watching her sisters strolling around with their own little chicks, she observed a tiny dark spot way up in the distance. She squinted and watched as the form became clearer and bigger. She had never seen that figure before. As she enquired of a family member close by what it was, he responded that he saw nothing but clouds. She almost forgot that she was accused of hallucinating many

12

times as she often saw things way off in the distance that her family members couldn't see.

Her vision was impeccable, but she was told that this was abnormal for a chicken. Hence, she thought something was wrong with her for possessing this ability. This was just one of the many reasons they couldn't relate to her.

As she gazed upon the form, she realized that it was getting closer and closer. Why did it seem like this creature was heading in her direction? She looked to see if any of her siblings saw the form heading towards the barn, but they all seemed to be unaware. She wanted to scream and tell them to run for cover, but for some strange reason she felt excitement and acute anticipation as the form came closer, flying directly towards her.

It was not until the figure, which was now clearly a big bird about her size, was about to land close by her that her chicken family scurried away and ran for cover. She initially felt like running with them and help shield them from this strange creature, but something about this fierce, beautiful (she must admit), strong, alluring bird excited and appealed to her. She just stood there gazing as he looked on her in wonderment.

She looked in his eyes and saw a hint of astonishment and skepticism. As she looked back in defiance, she saw a glimmer of compassion then amusement in his eyes as the outstanding bird standing in front of her stretched out his magnificent wings with utmost confidence and regality.

She looked on in admiration as her wings itched to feel the freedom his action seemed to evoke. She had never stretched out her wings like that before. She always thought that her wings were too big and feared they would hurt one of her family members if she tried to stretch them out in the small space they occupied. Worse, she dreaded the notion that they may just laugh at her size as she was told that she was too big and awkward. As she resisted the urge to spread her wings like the magnificently exquisite creature standing before her, she noticed that he was the same size as she was. For the first time she was seeing a chicken that looked just like her, she thought.

He looked on in amazement as she gawked over him. He then interrupted her gaze spell as he said to her in the most soothing tone, "I have been watching you from the clouds for a while now. You don't belong here. You believe you are a chicken, but you are really an EAGLE. I am here to help you find the strength of your wings, to activate your natural eagle instincts so you can take your rightful place as QUEEN in the sky and be the great and magnificent creature you were made to be. I will show you how to spread your wings, to take off and take your rightful place. I will show you how to hunt for real food and how to take care of yourself and your young ones. I know that all your life you were treated and told you were a chicken, but you are an eagle and it is now time for you to assert and accept your GREATNESS."

Like Nia, so many of us were born eagles but somehow thought we were chickens. We were created and endowed with exceptional and exquisite gifts, but our circumstances prevented us from fully activating our eagle instincts. This 21-day devotional is uniquely designed for SUPER women who know what it is like to:

1. feel odd or different.
2. be criticized, ostracized and attacked.
3. feel inadequate, incompetent and unworthy.
4. feel sad, broken and rejected.
5. feel burdened with guilt, shame and stagnation.
6. wait, suffer long and constantly desire more.
7. feel tired, drained, empty and hopeless.

This book was penned with the intention of reminding super women that they have an incomprehensibly, inexhaustibly, boundlessly, enormous amount of strength, vigor, vivacity and vitality encoded in their chromosomal composition; specially programmed by the Creator from conception.

Before I formed thee in the belly I knew thee; and before you camest forth out of the womb I sanctified thee; and I ordained thee. (Jeremiah 1:5).

All that is required is that she daily stimulate her power through quiet contemplation of the Word, humble and hushed meditation, selfless reflection and earnest supplication remembering that:

> *He giveth power to the faint; and to them that have no might he increaseth strength. (Isaiah 40:29).*

This divinely inspired devotional is designed to motivate, challenge, soothe, stir, enthuse, encourage, embolden and evoke a longing within every woman who reads it to draw strength and inspiration from the Word of God and tap into her eagle instincts in order to overcome the daily challenges, attacks and insecurities that plague her in an imperfect world so she can *"...mount up with wings like an Eagle..." (Isaiah 40:31).*

The contents of this book are meant to be relished and savored. It is really one bowl of sweet savory nuggets that you take once daily. This unique devotional style will stimulate the palate of your "mind buds" and leave you feeling full and satisfied as you feed on the nutritious spiritual ingredients that will strengthen your wings for flight.

Chapter 1

Feeling Odd or Different

Nia spent her whole life feeling different from everyone around her. She looked, sounded, walked, talked and thought differently because she was indeed different. She was an eagle raised among chickens.

Even though she was different, she desired desperately to be ordinary so she could fit in with everyone around her. Her desire was to be accepted and be liked by everyone. She didn't realize that even though circumstances had brought her to the barn, her calling and purpose was not for or of the barn.

Sadly, her difference brought her pain and sadness. For a time, she was made to feel that being different was wrong. She didn't know her worth or purpose and those around her were also unaware of this purpose. They just knew that it made them feel uncomfortable and it intimidated them.

Sounds familiar? Is this relatable? If you can relate to Nia's experience, I would like to advise and assure you of three things:

1. You were CALLED and CHOSEN to be different.

2. You need to embrace and treasure your authenticity.
3. You need to know and accept the fact that not everyone will appreciate you being different and authentic.

Day 1

CALLED and CHOSEN to be Different

Affirmation

I am different because I am CALLED, CHOSEN, ordained and set aside for a holy PURPOSE.

But ye are a chosen generation, a royal priesthood, an holy nation, a peculiar people... (1 Peter 2:9).

It is not uncommon for a child of God to feel odd or different. Like Nia, this sensitivity may leave you with an instinctive desire to try and fit in. This is so because two bi-products of being different and outstanding are solitude and isolation. But God calls you to stand firm and know that you *"...are called according to His purpose." (Romans 8:28)*.

Joseph, David, Daniel, Shadrach, Meshach and Abednego are just a few of the distinguished Bible characters we can consider when we speak about being the odd one out, or the one sticking out in a crowd, which is, having differing beliefs, endowed with special gifts or being called and chosen for a particular purpose.

We see how they felt lonely and isolated in their respective plots, but they recognized that their purpose far exceeded how others viewed them. They knew they were chosen for a higher calling and this recognition emboldened them to walk with assurance into the marvelous light that beckoned.

Nothing is wrong with feeling odd or being different. Not only are you different from over seven billion plus people in the world, but the sperm that collided with your mother's ovum was a winning sperm that won the race with 499,999,999 other sperms that were racing to fertilize your mother's egg. Yes, your father expelled half a billion minuscule reproductive cells inside your mother, and you topped the race and overcome over-whelming odds to be here. You are a miracle! You are chosen!

The Word of God declares that you are royal, peculiar and called for a special and unique function. God designed you to be different; to carry out a particular purpose. He fashioned you artfully and masterfully from conception, then endowed you with authentic gifts to glorify Him and bequeath the world with your exquisite authenticity. You are not your own, for *ye are bought with a price (See 1 Corinthians 6:20).*

He has a special and unique plan for your life and that is why He has CALLED you, not your 499,999,999 sisters or brothers who didn't make it here, but YOU! Too often we forget, so Jesus reminds us in His Word that, "*Ye have not chosen me, but I have chosen you, and ordained you, that ye should go and bring forth fruit." (John 15:16).*

Today, remind yourself that even though you may experience isolation and loneliness because you are different from those around you, you have a special and distinct calling on your life. You are chosen of the Lord. You did not choose Him, He chose YOU!

Eagle Instinct: Birdwatchers and Scientists initially concluded that there are roughly between 9,000 and 10,000 species of birds in the world. Recent studies have made an estimation that this number may have escalated to possibly 18,000. The eagle specie has maintained its place as the grandest and most magnificent and awe-inspiring of birds. They are different and stands out among all the other bird species. The eagle was designed by the Creator to standout in every way. All the features and characteristics of the eagle are impressive and are likened to strength, regality, power and vigor. Nia was an eagle and eagles are not made to co-exist with chickens. You have within you an inner eagle that makes you exquisite and rare. Like Nia, you stand out among those around you because you were designed to be GREAT and achieve amazing things.

Prayer:

Abba, Father, I am so grateful that You created me different. Help me to recognize that I am special, unique and authentic and that You have called, chosen, ordained and set me apart for a holy purpose. Reveal my purpose and help me to consistently do Your will. Amen.

Day 2

Embrace And Treasure Your Authenticity

Affirmation

I am a unique and authentic masterpiece, meticulously created by God!

Before I formed thee in the belly I knew thee; and before thou camest forth out of the womb I sanctified thee, and I ordained thee... (Jeremiah 1:5).

You may have heard before that "a gift is not a gift until it is accepted." God gifted you with authenticity, but you will never know the true value and worth until you have accepted and embraced it.

God took meticulous care when He formed and fashioned you in your mother's womb. Psalm 139:13 expresses that *"...thou hast possessed my reins: thou hast covered me in my mother's womb."*

There is no other soul on this earth who looks, speaks, thinks, acts or behaves like you. You were created with a uniquely patterned fingerprint and an exclusive iris prototype. Your features, personality and traits are a limited combination that is of an atypical edition.

Even if you are an identical twin, you are not the same. If for a minute you are tempted to entertain the thought of being common, average or regular, consider this:

> *But even the very hairs of your head are all numbered. Fear not therefore: ye are of more value than many sparrows. (Luke 12:7).*

Wow! Just imagine, God keeps an account of every solitary string of your hair. According to Scientists, your body contains approximately 37.2 trillion cells and God has a record of that too.

Consequently, you show appreciation and honor to the benefactor of this excellent gift of authenticity by treasuring it and by giving glory and honor to Him. Hence, like the Psalmist, you ought to daily affirm that:

> *I will praise thee; for I am fearfully and wonderfully made: marvelous are thy works; and that my soul knoweth right well. (Psalm 139:14).*

I challenge you today to meditate on these verses and remind yourself how unique, rare, distinguished and authentic you are in God's sight. He took special care in designing and creating you. So, you owe it to Him to acknowledge His masterpiece by embracing and acknowledging your uniqueness.

Eagle Instinct: Eagles are the most confident and graceful of birds. When an eagle is in flight, she exudes such confidence, grace and power that Proverbs 30:18-19 mentions that, *"There are three things which are too wonderful for me...the way of an eagle in the air..."* Eagles assert their authenticity and dominate any territory they occupy. You have the confidence and assurance that you are unique and, like the eagle, you need to boldly and graciously exude your authentic nature.

Nia wasn't aware of her magnificence because of her circumstance. Even though she knew she was different, she didn't understand that her difference made her superbly distinguished. Like Nia, your circumstances may have led you to feel less of who you really are but tap into your inner eagle and evoke every ounce of confidence befitting the unique being you were created to be.

Prayer:

Holy God, I am forever grateful for the unique fashioning of my life. You took great care in forming and putting together my inward and outward parts. I honor You with my entire being and ask that You will help me to acknowledge and rejoice in this authenticity as I use it for Your Glory. Amen.

Day 3

You Are Different And Authentic

Affirmation

I accept that others may not appreciate my unique gifts and character traits, but I love how I was fashioned and I choose to bask in my authenticity!

> *If the world hate you, ye know that it hated me before it hated you. (John 15:18).*

God, out of His just and generous nature, gave every single human being a selection of gifts, *"...differing according to the grace that is given to us..." (See Romans 12:6).* Not one single soul, no matter his/her condition, can assert that he/she is gift-less.

The problem though is expressed profoundly in the allusion that everyone is sitting at a dining table and served a unique dish. Some persons dig in and are enjoying the meal set before them, but some are unable to enjoy their meal because they are busy watching the plates of those sitting nearby. They are naïve to the fact that each meal is prepared specifically to satisfy the nutritional needs of the person it is served. Unfortunately, they are busy scrutinizing and comparing the quantity and quality,

26

not knowing that what they are served is perfectly prepared for them, taking into consideration their digestive makeup and tolerances. They are oblivious to the fact that partaking in someone else's dish could give them heartburn, indigestion or food poisoning.

Putting that into perspective, your gifts and abilities are unique to you. God, in His wisdom, issued to everyone according to his/her ability to handle, care and relate to that which is given. God's selection and serving process is far beyond human comprehension and intellectual grasp. His will and purpose is always supreme and incontestable.

Sadly, many are not satisfied with the distribution process. Hence, your gifts are enviable and may offend some persons. Some persons lack self-efficacy and confidence in themselves. They do not fully appreciate and value their uniqueness and the gifts they are given. As a result, they are overtaken with envy and bitterness because they believe they should be the recipient of the meal you are partaking of or the gifts you have. This causes them to neglect their own appetizing dish and become consumed with envy and spend their time undermining and undervaluing others.

Jesus endured much hostility, envy and hatred because of His peculiar nature. Isaiah tells us that, *"He is despised and rejected of men…" (Isaiah 53:3a).*

His presence and holy character made the Scribes and Pharisees and the proud in heart uncomfortable because His light exposed their inadequacies, insecurities, incompetences and proved them to be impostors. The devil planted seeds of jealousy, hatred, bitterness, envy and strife in their hearts so much that they wanted Him dead.

Similarly, the devil despises your gifts and uses whoever he may to undermine them. But Jesus left us with a blueprint to handle such nuances so we will not be affected or marred by negative assaults. He admonished:

> *If the world hate you, ye know that it hated me before it hated you. (John 15:18).*

When you acknowledge and accept the fact that not everyone will appreciate or even understand your exquisiteness, you will be ennobled with an elevated code of empathy and consideration that will shield and make you immune to such harmful reactions.

Therefore, because you have the advantage of knowing the behind-the-scenes plot in this matter, and because you are of a peculiar caliber, you have a responsibility to treat your detractors with the elevated, neutralizing reaction of LOVE. Jesus Himself instructed us to, *"Love your enemies, bless them that curse you, do good to them that hate you, and pray for them which despitefully use you, and persecute you." (Matthew 5:44).* Use your gifts and special abilities to show them that they are special too.

Shine your light so it can bless and influence them positively.

I challenge you today to pray for those who treat you unkindly or undermine you because of your uniqueness.

Eagle Instinct: An eagle is not intimidated by any other species. They are always up for a challenge. They know there are many animals that are not fond of them or appreciate their magnificence, for example, the serpent.

Nia's upbringing with chickens limited her ability to exude her confidence. She allowed the way those around her responded to her uniqueness to affect her, because she did not know she was an eagle. Like Nia, you may feel intimidated by others around you who despise your authenticity, but when you accept that this is a natural reaction from those who are insecure, you will boldly and confidently assert your unique abilities because you are born to be great just like an eagle.

Prayer:

Mighty God, I recognize that the devil doesn't like the fact that I am Yours and that You have called and equipped me for a purpose. I know he will use persons to undermine my gifts. I pray that You will shield and strengthen me to overcome these challenges and not allow them to affect my confidence and calling. I leave it all in Your hand! In Jesus' name. Amen.

Chapter 2

To Be Criticized, Ostracized And Attacked

Nia was heavily criticized by her family. She was ostracized and attacked on numerous occasions. In chapter one, it was established that she was seen as different and odd because she was of a different make and model from those around her. Even the impressive gifts she possessed were diminished and disregarded. Her positive attributes were held in a negative light.

The anointing on your life that accompanies your chosen and called status will attract much criticism and attacks in the same manner that light attracts bugs and moths. You may have your character disfigured or assassinated just because you are unique. You will face various spiritual and temporal assaults, and even encounter levels of alienation and separation.

In the introductory anecdote, Nia was unjustly criticized, and her competences were lessened and treated as if they were liabilities rather than assets. Even though she was larger in size, her siblings teamed up against her and attacked and alienated her. This aroused self-doubt and left her entertaining thoughts of being abnormal and unworthy and even questioning her purpose and value.

Sounds familiar? Do you know anyone who may have experienced similar treatment from persons in their families, at work, school, in their community or even in their church? Can you relate in any way? I would like to assure and caution you that:

1. Your calling will attract attacks.
2. Trust the process.
3. You are not forsaken.

Day 4

Your CALLING Attracts Attacks

Affirmation

I am called and chosen for a purpose and I will not fall prey to the attacks of the enemy.

> *Rejoice, and be exceeding glad: for great is your reward in heaven: for so prosecuted they the prophets which were before you. (Matthew 5:12).*

A thorough and comprehensive search of the Bible would yield that not one human being who was called and purposed by God was spared some form of attack or persecution. Our first lady, Eve, mother of all generations, was pursued by the devil and had her divine purpose compromised in such a severe manner that hundreds of centuries later we are still paying the consequences for the result of that first attack.

Satan, from time immemorial, has been devising schemes and plots to undermine God's plan of salvation, and everyone who is branded and wears the seal of God is automatically a prime candidate for his onslaughts.

Consequently, simply being a child of God, called and chosen to fulfill His divine function, will incite satan to round up a troop to torment, criticize, ostracize, accuse and attack your calling and purpose.

While Jesus was here, He, the Creator and sustainer of the world, was heavily and strongly accused. He was even regarded as being a mad man. This is possibly one of the most degrading labels one can affix to anyone's character. He was spoken about negatively and He was indicted as a criminal. Everything He did was scrutinized and criticized. And so, He cautions us that, *"The servant is not greater than his lord. If they persecuted me, they will also persecute you." (See John 15:20).*

He also gives us the reassurance that once we do His will, there is a sure reward for us, *"Blessed are they which are persecuted for righteousness sake: for theirs is the kingdom of heaven." (Matthew 5:10).*

You may be unaware of your true purpose, but I guarantee you have an exquisite purpose to fulfill in this life and it threatens the devil's kingdom, and it may also intimidate someone.

You may have heard the saying that, "Thieves don't break into empty houses. The thief wouldn't be attacking you if something valuable wasn't inside you." Therefore, you need to be aware that you are being attacked, criticized and ostracized because of the treasure that is within you. So, you have to, *"Be sober, be vigilant; because your adversary the devil, as a roaring lion, walketh about seeking whom he may devour." (1 Peter 5:8).*

It is, therefore, imperative that you equip yourself in order to combat these attacks by remaining steadfast, pray earnestly, study and live the WORD and constantly affirm yourself with Paul's declaration that, *"I press toward the mark for the prize of the high calling of God in Christ Jesus."(Philippians 3:14).*

You need to be assured that:

> *The angel of the Lord encampeth round about them that fear him, and delivereth them. (Psalm 34:7).*

Eagle Instinct: The serpent, as mentioned before, is one of the few creatures brazen enough to confront the eagle. The eagle knows that the serpent has sneaky and devious tendencies. Hence, it is always mindful and alert when it is grounded knowing that the attack from a serpent is probable. She is, therefore, very cautious.

Whenever an attack is launched, she acts swiftly by grabbing the serpent's tail or body and ascends into the sky at rocket speed taking him to high altitudes where it is impossible for him to breathe. Within seconds, the serpent succumbs, and she releases its corpse to the ground.

Nia's attack was of a milder nature. Chickens, pigeons and other insignificant birds could never intimidate an eagle under normal circumstances. When persons display chicken tendencies, for example, gossiping, squabbling and pointing fingers at you, the eagle in you should not be affected or tempted to respond. However, when the attacks intensify, like the eagle, fight your enemies in a higher realm. Don't face him in his comfort zone in the carnal. Take it up in prayer where he is powerless and is already defeated.

Prayer:

Mighty God, I recognize that the treasure You have placed within me will constantly attract attacks until that day You usher me to Your heavenly kingdom. I pray that You will dispatch a special army of angels to protect and deliver me from these attacks. Help me to be always mindful of the fact that You will never give me more than I can bear and that You overcame so that I can overcome. Thank You for hearing and answering my prayers. In Jesus' name. Amen.

Day 5

Trust The Process

Affirmation

I am unique and called for a special purpose, which makes me susceptible to attacks. I will trust the process knowing that it is for my edification.

Thou hast beset me behind and before, and laid thine hand upon me. (Psalm 139:5).

We would never know, recognize and appreciate the goodness of God, if we never knew hardship, attacks and tribulation.

Abraham would never be the Father of faith, nor Joseph the powerful pardoning Prime Minister. Job would never be the epitome of endurance, neither would Paul be the paragon of persecution turned prolific preacher. Moses would never be the master of meekness nor David the Distinguished Director of the divinely appointed dynasty. We would never identify the need of God as the Savior, Sustainer and Deliverer, if we never truly endured some ordeal of distress, destitution or dissonance in our lives. We would never get a chance to prove ourselves worthy of the calling on our lives. As *"Every man's work shall be made manifest: for the day shall declare it, because it shall be revealed by fire; and the fire shall try every man's work of what sort it is." (1 Corinthians 3:13).*

It was never God's intention for us to suffer pain and affliction, but with the advent of the fall, satan's determination has been to wreak mayhem and havoc. Our only defense is in the safety of the Savior. But we are encouraged to, *"...count it all joy when ye fall into divers temptations; knowing this, that the trying of your faith worketh patience." (James 1:2-3).*

The strengthening and perfecting of our characters, to reach heavenly standards, to make us worthy of our calling, is found in the testing of our faith. Patience is both a virtue and a requirement necessary to truly attain the highest possible and most desirable of divine standards. James corroborates, *"But let patience have her perfect work, that ye may be perfect and entire, wanting nothing."(James 1:4).*

The standard of heaven is perfection and holiness, and this is achieved when we have endured, like Jesus, the tests and attacks that are aimed at us. Christ assured us that, *"...My grace is sufficient for thee: for my strength is made perfect in weakness." (See 2 Corinthians 12:9).*

Therefore, like Paul, declare, *"...I take pleasure in infirmities, in reproaches, in necessities, in persecutions, in distresses for Christ's sake: for when I am weak, then am I strong. (2 Corinthians 12:10).*

With each test that we overcome, the muscle of our faith, much like physical exercising, is toned and grows stronger and stronger until we reach the ultimate goal.

In each test and attack there is an opportunity, a lesson and a reward:

- **An opportunity** to call upon God, to glorify Him and show gratitude when He delivers us.

- **A lesson** for ourselves and others to learn, so that we can be victors. When we depend on God totally, He will help us to deal with, prevent and endure future distress.

- **The reward** is an incredible, accolade of achievement of having survived and surmounted the attack.

Thus, Paul was on point when he declared, *"...that all things work together for good to them that love God, to them who are called according to his purpose. (Romans 8:28).*

Your attacks will make you stronger and wiser. All the noble Patriarchs mentioned earlier experienced varied levels of attacks, criticism and being ostracized. However, it all *"worked together for good."* Their characters were refined through the process and made them the heroic champions of faith they were, revealing the glory of God. In like manner, *"...rejoice, in as much as ye are partakers* of Christ's sufferings; that, when his glory shall be revealed, ye may be glad also with exceeding joy." (1 Peter 4:13).

Accordingly, we truly become a friend of God and make Him proud when we go through the process without giving up or folding. We prove ourselves to be "more than conquerors" when our lives are refined through the process and we can assert, "For thou, O God, has proved us: thou hast tried us, as silver is tried." (Psalms 66:10).

I, therefore, challenge you today to identify the opportunity, the lesson and the possible reward in the attacks, knowing that in the end you will be a conqueror when your calling is made manifest. Trust the process!

Eagle Instinct: If any other creature knows the value of a process, it is the eagle. The eagle endures various processes in their subsistence and overall lives that are critical to their survival. Their characters were designed in a sophisticated manner where principle and strict discipline are traits necessary to sustain their existence.

One such process is what I call the "attraction initiation." The attraction initiation requires the male eagle to prove himself worthy of the female's affection and attention. He is put through a test to prove his loyalty, agility and determination. The female flies to the ground with her suitor in hot pursuit and picks up a twig. She then flies to a high altitude and he follows her. When she has reached a certain level, she drops the twig and the male eagle swoops down and catches it and proudly returns it to her. She goes to a higher altitude and repeats this action and he pursues it and takes it back to her. She does this several times for hours, each time increasing altitude until she is satisfied that he has satisfactorily proven the desired traits, proving his worth.

In similar manner, we are tested so we can prove our love, loyalty and devotion to our Savior, who laid down His life in our stead. Catching the twig may seem a tiresome task, especially after doing it repeatedly, but the reward is worth the process. We become stronger and get to spend eternity with our Savior, after we have persevered and won the race of life.

Prayer:

Holy Father, how excellent is Your name! I honor and glorify You because You are worthy. I recognize that testing is a critical part of the process of refining my life for a higher calling and so I will be susceptible to criticism, attacks, and being ostracized as You were when You were here. Please help me to look beyond the discomfort and pain and trust the process. In Jesus' name I pray. Amen.

Day 6

You Are Not Forsaken

Affirmation

I am covered, protected and sanctified. The Lord has a great plan for my life. Therefore, even though I face trials, I am not forsaken.

I have been young, and now am old; yet have I not seen the righteous forsaken, nor his seed begging bread. (Psalm 37:25).

Have you ever felt the weight of the world pressing brutally on the crown of your head as if to crush you to smithereens? Have you ever felt like you are squared in, trapped between the pressures of converging walls? Have you ever felt like your life is a constant battle between yourself and dragons where you have to be relentlessly dodging the fire spewed at you?

Heavy weight, crashing walls and fiery dragons are just a few of the analogies we can ascribe to our experiences of being cursed, hated and despitefully used. However, *"We are troubled on every side, yet not distressed; we are perplexed but not in despair; persecuted but not forsaken; cast down, but not destroyed." (2 Corinthians 4:8-9).*

Ever so often, a child of God who is called and chosen may be attacked, criticized and ostracized. When such trials press and distress, it is tempting to think that you are forsaken. This dark period during the battle may cause you to wonder for a moment if you can survive or bear it. But you have the assurance that, "...*the Lord is faithful, who shall stablish you, and keep you from evil.*" *(2 Thessalonians 3:3).*

Hence, no matter the propensity of the pressures or the intensity of the fiery darts, "...*the Lord...doth go before thee; he will be with thee, he will not fail thee, neither forsake thee: fear not, neither be dismayed. (Deuteronomy 31:8).*

The Bible is punctuated with the most beautiful promises and assurances to perfume the soul of the one who is encumbered, aggrieved and distraught from mean, maligning, malicious, verbal assaults, cold, cruel claws of criticism or overt onslaughts of exclusion, separation and segregation. In Christ, the Word, we can find an asylum of peace, assurance, comfort, consolation and defense: a refuge! For "*God is our refuge and strength, a ever present help in trouble.*" *(Psalm 46:1).*

Mary Magdalene was heavily criticized and maligned and, although she was presumably guilty, the Master did not forsake her. Even though she was attacked and ostracized for the sins she committed, she was not scorned by the Holy of Holies and she was not treated as a cast away. Jesus proved a defense and refuge for her when the menacing crowd spat offensive and demeaning words and were ready to take her life. He spoke to her in a calm, soothing voice after enquiring of her accusers, *"...Neither do I condemn thee: go and sin no more." (John 8:11b).*

Hannah, on the other hand, was more of an innocent. She was scorned and ridiculed by her adversary, Peninnah, who took no pains in ridiculing and provoking her. She was a *"woman of a sorrowful spirit."* But the Lord heard and delivered her so that she was able to proclaim, *"...My heart rejoiceth in the Lord, mine horn is exalted in the Lord: my mouth is enlarged over mine enemies; because I rejoice in thy salvation."(1 Samuel 2:1).*

That is the nature of the God we serve. Whether you are an innocent or condemned, He will rescue and deliver you from your enemies. For *"He hath not dealt with us after our sins; nor rewarded us according to our iniquities." (Psalms 103:10).*

It doesn't matter if the world thinks you are undeserving of grace and mercy, and take pleasure in hurling insults at you, you are not forsaken by your Creator. The prophet declares, *"Thou shalt no more be termed Forsaken; neither shall thy land be termed Desolate: but thou shalt be called...for the Lord delighteth in thee..." (Isaiah 62:4).*

Therefore, when your soul is tormented and it seems like the world is against you; when those you hold dear have rejected and scornfully used and abused you; when your efforts are ridiculed and treated with contempt, know that your Lord is waiting to soothe the raw wounds of your hurt, to pacify your burning soul, to relieve the aching of your heart and calm the racing of your mind. He is a balm, a shelter and, as David beautifully expressed, *"Thou art my hiding place; thou shalt preserve me from trouble; thou shalt compass me about with songs of deliverance. Selah." (Psalm 32:7).*

Thus, I challenge you to assert, *"Though I walk in the midst of trouble, thou wilt revive me. Thou shalt stretch forth thine hand against the wrath of mine enemies, and thy right hand shall save me." (Psalms 138:7).*

Eagle Instinct: In Exodus 19:4, the Lord pronounced, *"...I bare you on eagles' wings, and brought you unto myself."* The eagle is highly regarded by the Creator. He designed them with magnificent wings to soar above the clouds. Eagles have the capacity to soar the highest of altitudes among the bird species. The eagle is not afraid of heights, obviously, and takes pride in elevation. They can fly to altitudes of over 10,000 feet.

If the Lord declares that He will bare you up on eagle's wings and bring you unto Himself, you can discard any notion of being forsaken.

Nia felt the brunt of isolation, criticism and felt forsaken because she wasn't aware of the power in her wings. She wasn't aware that she had the capacity to fly out of the coop, above the barn and unto greater heights; to altitudes where her chicken counterparts couldn't see her much less to forsake her. You have the capacity and ability to fly above your oppressors and anything that causes you to feel forsaken. Your power is in your wings. As you grow stronger in Christ, you will find the power the Holy Ghost imbues you with shall enable you *"to mount up with wings as eagles."*

Prayer:

Father God, I yearn to grow stronger in You. Your words have established that I am not forsaken, and I am most delighted to know that You have extended Your grace and mercy towards me. Thank You for Your leading and direction. Amen.

Chapter 3

To Feel Sad, Broken And Rejected

The mechanical or human response to destructive criticism, excessive attacks and isolation are sadness, brokenness and rejection. These emotions were evident in Nia's narrative, and they are emotions that are relatable to the human experience.

Everyone has experienced some form of sadness, brokenness and encountered some level of rejection at some point in their lives. We don't always get the things we desire; life doesn't always go the way we planned, and we experience loss and hurt of some kind along the way.

Nia was bound, or so she thought, by physical space. The environment and her family were a constant reminder that she didn't belong there. Nothing she did seemed right in their sight and her refusal to participate in their negative past-time of squabbling and gossiping only added fuel to the fire and acid to the wound. It made them angry towards Nia, which in turn made her sad, broken-spirited and rejected.

Similarly, many of us are bound to a physical space and are constantly around people who make us feel sad, broken and rejected; whether it is in our homes, at work, school or in our communities.

I want to assure you, however, that you can find PEACE, and when you encounter feelings of sadness, brokenness or rejection, you don't have to succumb to their destructive consequences. There is always a way of escape. I encourage you to:

1. Lift up your eyes.
2. Search, find and adhere to the Word.
3. Pray incessantly.

Day 7

Lift Up Your Eyes

Affirmation

I lift up my eyes to God because I know He will take care of my every need and deliver me from sorrow, brokenness and rejection.

> *I will lift up mine eyes unto the hills, from whence cometh my help. My help cometh from the Lord, which made heaven and earth. He will not suffer thy foot to be moved: he that keepeth thee will not slumber. (Psalm 121:1-3).*

David penned many comforting, soul-stirring and thrilling Psalms, but he certainly outdid himself with this one.

When our souls are distressed, when it is in torment, this is a beautiful Psalm that can give sweet assurance, joy, hope and elevate us from a state of self-pity and drudgery, to one of excellence and victory. Jesus says, *"Come unto me, all ye that labor and are heavy laden, and I will give you rest. For my yoke is easy, and my burden is light."* (Matthew 11:28 & 30).

We don't need to go on a wild goose chase to seek happiness and comfort, when the source is literally in us and in constant reach: God. We are encouraged to, *"Draw nigh to God, and he will draw nigh to you." (James 4:8a).* We need no device to access Him, just one simple action; "a lift": a lift of our eyes, a lift of our minds or a lift of our hearts and He will come to our rescue and allow His transforming power to permeate the dark recesses of our soul and bathe us in the perfume and light of his LOVE. All He asks is, *"Be still, and know that I am God." (Psalms 46:10a).*

When we lift our eyes, hearts and minds to Him, it communicates three things:

- **Surrender:** We are telling God that we are depending totally on Him; that we recognize that we cannot sustain ourselves. It is a display of humility and God delights in a humble heart and a contrite spirit. The Word invites us to, *"Humble yourselves therefore under the mighty hand of God, that He may exalt you in due time: Casting all of your care upon Him; for he careth for you." (1 Peter 5:6-7).* When we surrender, we release the hold on the steering of our lives and give Him full authority to have His own way and to have His will manifest in us. He invites us to, *"...call upon me in the day of trouble: I will deliver thee, and thou shalt glorify me. (Psalms 50:15).*

- **Renunciation:** When we lift up our eyes, we indicate that we are willing and ready to renounce our sinful ways. *"...Cleanse your hands, ye sinners; and purify your hearts..." (See James 4:8),* knowing that *"He that covereth His sins shall not prosper: but whoso confesseth and forsaketh them shall have mercy."(Proverbs 28:13).* We must be willing to confess and repent of our sins so that God can have His perfect way in us and give us the desires of our hearts.

- **Trust:** Lifting up our eyes is an indicator that we trust God. Solomon advises, *"Trust in the Lord with all thine heart; and lean not unto thine own understanding. In all thy ways acknowledge him, and he shall direct thy paths." (Proverbs 3:5-6).* When we lift up our eyes, we are telling Him in a nonverbal manner that we acknowledge Him as sovereign and trust Him to direct our paths. We are also professing boldly that, *"In thee, O Lord, do I put my trust; let me never be ashamed: deliver me in thy righteousness." (Psalm 31:1).*

He knows the language of your heart. He can decode every emotion and interpret every tear that falls from your eyes. Long before your tear is produced in your lacrimal gland and drains through your tear ducts, He sent angels to comfort you and soothe your soul.

Next time you feel sad, lonely, broken and rejected, just lift your eyes, heart and mind towards heaven from whence cometh your help because God longs to deliver you. He longs to rescue, restore and replenish your joy stock. It is not His will that we should be afflicted in sorrow, grief and depression all our lives. He desires for us to live a cheerful and fulfilling life.

> *And he shall be like a tree planted by the rivers of waters, that bringeth forth his fruit in his season; his leaf also shall not wither; and whatsoever he doeth shall prosper. (Psalms 1:3).*

Eagle Instinct: Nia tried hanging her head in the peak of her sorrow, but it was not in her nature to do so. She, instead, found herself gazing in the sky where her redemption would be found. The sky is where the eagle finds freedom. This is where they get to express and exhibit their grandeur, to glide through the clouds and catch a glimpse of the earth's splendor.

Like the eagle, our freedom, hope, restoration and redemption are up above. Father God, the Omnipotent One who resides in the Heavenly Courts, desires for us to look to Him for help when we are suffering from affliction, pain, scorn, sorrow and grief. He longs to have us glide in our freedom. He longs to give us wings so we can mount up like eagles and catch a glimpse of the splendor of His hands. He longs to relieve us from the bondages, chains and shackles that have us grounded.

Raise your chin, Eagle Queen, lift up your head and look to the hills and the skies from where your help comes.

Prayer:

Friend of a wounded heart, I lift my eyes to You because I know that all my hope, joy, peace and comfort can be found in You. It is in You that I put my trust. I renounce my sins and surrender my all. Lift me up and cause me to fly on eagle's wings. To You I give all honor, glory and praise. Amen.

Day 8

Search, Find And Adhere To The Word

Affirmation

I will search, find and adhere to the Word, for in it there is light, life and love to heal, purify and cleanse my soul.

This is my comfort in my affliction: for thy word hath quickened me. (Psalm 119:50).

The world has been scoured over thoroughly for the evidence of one written document, literary compilation or scripted composition that can be compared to the Word of God. This has proven to be an effort most futile. No other epistle, chronicle, narrative, journal or volume is as complete, endearing, edifying, satisfying, descriptive, prescriptive, encouraging, intriguing, fulfilling, comforting, stimulating or captivating as the written, divinely inspired Word of God.

If you are hungry, it nourishes your spirit. If you thirst, it refreshes and satisfies your soul. If you are sick, in it you will find healing. If you are dull, in it is a wellspring of knowledge and wisdom. If you lack love, you will find the Author of love and light. If you are bored, it is sure to entertain you. If you long for drama, it is loaded with every possible form. If you desire to prosper, it is the hallmark for progressive living.

If you are lost, in it you will find direction. Tormented? It is a book of peace. If you are in need, it will help you bridge your lack. Lonely? In it you find comfort. Most importantly, if you desire to know the love and companionship of the Creator, Sustainer and Deliverer of the Universe, He is the manifested Word. He is the protagonist, the focus, the epicenter of it all.

Therefore, a sure repellant for the gloom that accompanies sadness, brokenness and rejection, and a guarantee of absolute hope, is a thorough and sincere exploration of the Word. The Word needs no validation, confirmation, justification or corroboration from any outside source as it absolutely proves itself word for word, line for line, and precept upon precept. It is the only book that transcends time, language and culture, testifies of the Creator and promises hope of life eternal. It therefore confirms, *"Search the scriptures; for in them ye think ye have eternal life: and they are they which testify of me." (John 5:39).*

The written Word of God is the medium and channel through which the God of all creation speaks to His children. The Word admonishes, purifies, and cleanses the parched, broken, vulnerable, sin-sick soul. If you desire complete healing and cleansing, it has the best prescription, *"Wherewithal shall a young man cleanse his*

way? By taking heed thereunto according to thy word."
(Psalms 119:9).

It is a sure light that directs and brightens the path of those who seek to walk steadfastly.

> *Thy word is a lamp unto my feet, and a light unto my path. (Psalms 119:105).*

It dispels fear:

> *For God hath not given us the spirit of fear; but of power, and of love and of a sound mind. (2 Timothy 1:7).*

It has the most appetizing nuggets that cheer up the palate of the mind.

> *Man shall not live by bread alone, but by every word that proceedeth out of the mouth of God. (Matthew 4:4b).*

This bread is the best remedy to settle, sustain and soothe the soul.

Consequently, seeking the presence of God and engaging Him through the Word early in the morning is the best foundation one could set for their day and the best curtains to close off an episode of work or play. It will surely keep at bay the demonic forces that are behind the sensations of brokenness, sadness and the lingering feelings of rejection that haunts the soul. It is most beautiful when one can assert, *"O thou art my God; early will I seek thee:*

my soul thirsteth for thee, my flesh longeth for thee in a dry and thirsty land, where no water is." (Psalm 63:1).

He has already assured us that, "...ye shall seek me, and find me, when ye shall search for me with all your heart." (Jeremiah 29:13).

He gives the promise that if we seek after Him, by searching the Word and adhering to the principles, that we shall have no form of lack, "The young lions do lack, and suffer hunger; but they that seek the Lord shall not want any good thing."(Psalm 34:10).

There is absolutely no loss in seeking the Lord through His Word. There is only incredible benefits and advantage to be derived from searching, finding and adhering to His Word. The balm and healing for any feeling of sadness, brokenness or rejection can be found therein. In fact, a blessing is proclaimed on those who indulge:

> Blessed are they that keep his testimonies, and that seek him with the whole heart. They also do no iniquity: they walk in his ways. (Psalm 119:2-3).

Eagle Instinct: The Word testifies of the importance, strength and magnificence of the eagle. God pays tribute to this profoundly amazing creature that was called into existence by Him. Commendable reference, allusions and mention has been made of the eagle in the Bible. Job enquired, "Doth the eagle mount up at thy command, and make her nest on high?" (Job 39:27).

There is so much to learn and assimilate from these references. Nia's experience, her circumstance and all that she endured, is quite relatable to the human experience, and reminds us of our need of a Savior. We know He will lift us up on eagle's wings and draw us closer to Him.

Prayer:

Almighty God, I desire to hide Your Word in my heart so that I may not sin against You. I know Your words will soothe and restore my soul. I ask that You create in me a hunger and a thirst so that I will feed upon it. Give me an appetite for heavenly things. Create in me a yearning to know more of You. Stimulate my mind and evoke a desire in me to draw close and feed upon Your life-giving words. Amen!

Day 9

Pray Incessantly

Affirmation

I will pray without ceasing, knowing that the solution and remedy to my sadness, brokenness and feelings of rejection can be found in incessant and sincere prayer.

Pray without ceasing. (1 Thessalonians 5:17).

Prayer is the most potent and poignant pathway that points and pulls us into the powerful presence of the precious, pardoning Peace-Speaker.

As a child, we absolutely depended on our parents or caregiver to supply our every need; to care for us and provide complete protection. There was a period in our lives when our mothers, especially, could do no wrong for most of us. We had categorical trust and reliance on the one who fostered our entry in the world and were entrusted to keep us safe. Even in adulthood, many persons depend on their parents for advice and other forms of assistance.

But there is a point when we discover that our parents are mere mortals and they do not have all the answers or solutions to our problems. We learn that there is a higher Being than our parents and every single breathing and living creature depends on Him. Yet, because He cannot be seen by our imperfect human eyes, we fail to call upon Him incessantly as we should and trust Him to deliver and provide for our every need. Jesus challenges us in Matthew 7:11, *"If ye then, being evil, know how to give good gifts unto their children, how much more shall your father which is in heaven give good things to them that ask him?"*

Joseph M. Scriven, a trained teacher and preacher from Ireland, lost his fiancé to drowning a day before they got married. He then migrated to Canada and fell in love a second time, but his second fiancé fell ill and passed a week prior to their wedding. Instead of being bitter, considering the harsh hand that was dealt him, he took a vow of poverty and pledged to spend the remainder of his life as a woodcutter, taking care of the needs of the poor, handicapped and indigent, while maintaining what those who came into his company and were privileged to grace his presence described as a "buoyant spirit."

Word that his mother was ill came to him years later, but he was unable to visit her in Ireland, so he wrote a powerful poem to comfort her, which captured the nature of his life and how integral prayer was in his relationship with Jesus. It was later transposed in a song and is one of the most famous modern hymns today.

This song aptly captures the essence of how we treat the act of prayer:

"What a friend we have in Jesus
All our sins and griefs to bear!
What a privilege to carry
Everything to God in prayer!
Oh, what peace we often forfeit;
Oh, what needless pain we bear
All because we do not carry
Everything to God in prayer!"

God yearns for us to bring EVERYTHING to Him and cast all our cares upon Him. He desires to give us peace for our sadness, healing for our brokenness and acceptance for our rejection. He proclaims, *"If my people which are called by my name, shall humble themselves and PRAY, and seek my face, and turn from their wicked ways; then will I hear from heaven, and will forgive their sin, and will heal their land."(2 Chronicles 7:14).*

He will not withhold anything good from us, if we come to Him in faith and pray with sincerity. We have this confidence, *"…that, if we ask any thing according to his will, he heareth us." (1 John 5:14).*

His ear is especially inclined to those who are sad, broken and rejected.

He will regard the prayer of the destitute, and not despise their prayer. (Psalm 102:17).

The Lord is nigh unto all them that call upon him,
to all that call upon him in truth. (Psalm 145:18).

This call is sure and true. He awaits our earnest supplication as He enquires:

Is any among you afflicted? let him pray. (James
5:13a).

Praying always with all prayer and supplication in
the Spirit, and watching thereunto with all
perseverance and supplication for all saints.
(Ephesians 6:18).

We are required to pray with a humble and meek heart and attitude, knowing that we serve a holy and peculiar God who basks in sincerity and simplicity. We need not worry about sounding fancy or try to impress Him as He admonishes, *"...when ye pray, use not vain repetitions, as the heathen do: for they think that they shall be heard for their much speaking." (Matthew 6:7).*

I challenge you, therefore, to make prayer a lifestyle. Let it be an integral part of your existence. In the same manner, as you check up on a friend or family who is dear to you, develop and maintain a communication line with heaven, and pour out your heart to the One who desires desperately to give you your heart's desire.

Pray incessantly!

Eagle Instinct: Prayer, to us, is what wings are to an eagle. The eagle's wings lift and transport them to astounding heights way beyond the clouds. Our prayers can take us even higher, as it lifts us up to the heavenly courts. When eagles fly, they use little energy. As they soar to astounding heights, their wings allow them to glide through the air and cut through the clouds as they bask in the splendor of creation.

When we pray, we ought to feel light as we glide and release our burdens, cut through our problems and bask in the manifold blessings of the Lord. We are supposed to soar to new heights after every prayer encounter, and glide through life as we are sheltered under the wings of the most High. Do not rob yourself of this incredible opportunity. Activate your wings and pray incessantly.

Prayer:

Dear Lord, let my prayer be set forth before Thee as an incense; and the lifting up of my hands as the evening sacrifice. Deliver me from feelings of sadness and rejection. Fill me with Your love and confidence so that I can walk boldly and confidently knowing that I have a God who loves and adores me. Take full control of my life as I humbly yield to Your will. Amen.

Chapter 4

To Feel Inadequate, Incompetent And Unworthy

Nia was evidently more brilliant, talented and competent than her siblings. She possessed superior intellectual and analytical abilities and her motor skills were unmatched. She even had a more attractive and impressive appearance and physique. It is a no-brainer that an eagle is a more magnificent creature than a chicken.

However, being outnumbered and out-cultured and, I would say, de-powered, poor Nia was oblivious to her beauty and grandeur. She didn't know who she was.

This also made her unaware of her worth and value. Her standard of self was measured by the meter of her counterparts, and their standard was limited. She had no idea that she was of a superior echelon.

So it is that when we are not fully cognizant of our value, worth and significance, we sometimes feel inadequate, incompetent and unworthy. Sadly, we often allow persons of derisory and critical aptitude, who are mostly biased by their limited experiences and are sometimes plagued with low self-worth themselves, to label and impose their negligible opinions on us about our own abilities and capabilities. Very often, these views are coming from a place of hatred, envy, bitterness, confusion, jealousy or hurt.

In chapter one, our worth, value and authenticity were discussed extensively. We were reminded that we are designed with great care and meticulous precision. However, sometimes we are surrounded by persons who diminish our worth and make us blind to the obvious. In such circumstances it takes much effort on our part to truly appreciate that we are adequate, competent and worthy.

If you have been led to feel, in some point of your life, that you are inadequate, incompetent or unworthy, I want to encourage you to:

1. Make a radical shift.
2. Rely completely on God.
3. Glorify God with your gifts.

Day 10

Make A Radical Shift

Affirmation

I am determined to make a meaningful shift in my life, knowing that when I have a mind like Christ, I will not be plagued with feelings of inadequacy, insecurity or incompetence.

And be not conformed to this world: but be ye transformed by the renewing of your mind, that ye may prove what is that good, and acceptable, and perfect will of God. (Romans 12:2).

Many times in life we are plagued with feelings of insecurity, inadequacy and unworthiness. This is especially evident when we are thrust in environments where we do not get to exude our God-given gifts and abilities. A very smart person, unknown to me, once noted that: "Everybody is born a genius. But if you judge a fish by its ability to climb a tree, it will live its whole life believing that it is stupid."

Other times, we give into what Psychologists refer to as a critical inner voice, which is a cruel, self-sabotaging voice we possess that is turned against us. This voice is highly critical, negative and unconstructive.

It casts doubt on our abilities, undermines our desires, and convinces us to be paranoid and suspicious towards our selves. This anti-self fills our mind with critical self-analysis and self-sabotaging thoughts that lead us to hold back or steer away from our true goals.[1]

I want to remind you, however, that you are superbly gifted, capable and competent. I repeat, no one is born gift-less! No matter what you were told, or how you are treated by those around you, *"You were fearfully and wonderfully made" (See Psalm 139:14)*. You were equipped twice by your Creator; once when He made you and secondly when He died for you. Therefore, you need to proclaim with all confidence, boldness and assurance that, *"I can do all things through Christ who strengtheneth me." (Philippians 4:13)*.

A proven prescription to remedy the feelings of inadequacy, incompetence and unworthiness is a radical shift:

- **A shift of the mind:** *Let this mind be in you which was also of Christ Jesus. (Philippians 2:5)*.

---

[1]–Robert Firestone 2013 "Why We Get In Our Way" Study

- **A shift from negative self-talk and fear:** *For God has not given us a spirit of fear; but of power, and of love, and of a sound mind. (2 Timothy 1:7).*

- **A shift from feelings of worry and anxiety:** *My God shall supply all your need according to his riches in glory by Christ Jesus. (Philippians 4:19).*

- **A shift from worrying about what people will do, think or say.** Remember: *Ye are of God...and have overcome them: because greater is he that is in you, than he that is in the world. (1 John 4:4).*

- **A shift from self-doubt, uncertainty and double-mindedness:** *How long halt ye between two opinions? (See 1 Kings 18:21). Submit yourselves therefore to God. Resist the devil, and he will flee from you. Draw nigh to God, and he will draw nigh to you. Cleanse your hands, ye sinners; and purify your hearts, ye double minded. (James 4:7-8).*

- **A shift from self-reliance to complete dependence on God:** *Trust in the Lord with all thine heart; and lean not unto thine own understanding. In all thy ways acknowledge him, and he shall direct thy paths. (Proverbs 3:5-6).*

After making this shift, you will discover that God has equipped and purposed you to live a fulfilling and amazing life. The problem is, because we allow our physical environment, people's negative opinions and our critical inner voice to be amplified, we forget that, *"...with God nothing shall be impossible." (Luke 1:37).*

We often fail to recognize that the Lord is our defense and refuge and fail to assert, like David, that, *"The Lord is my light and my salvation; whom shall I fear? The Lord is the strength of my life; of whom shall I be afraid?" (Psalm 27:1).*

Therefore, you are capable, adequate, gifted, BLESSED and highly favored. You are called, chosen and equipped and God has a beautiful plan for your life to prosper and elevate you. Remember, *"With men this is impossible; but with God all things are possible." (Matthew 19:26b).*

Eagle Instinct: Eagles are bold and confident. They love challenges. In the midst of a challenge, they get to prove that they are competent and worthy to be master of the sky. One of the greatest challenges that an eagle faces boldly and excitedly is the storm.

While other birds scurry for cover, the eagle, sensing that a storm is coming, elevates her mind, shifts her attitude and aptitude and allows the storm to lift her to higher altitudes. She uses the force of the storm to glide above the raging tempests until it ceases. She never once doubts whether her wings would be able to sustain as she uses the energy of the storm to keep her wings aloft.

So it is that when we are faced with the storms of life, when we are confronted with challenges of all sorts, we ought to shift our mindset from a chicken to that of an eagle. Shift our minds and attitude and go to a higher level than our problems, trusting that God will keep us elevated no matter how long the problems, attacks or inconveniences last. Declare boldly that, "I am Competent, Adequate, Capable, Worthy and I can do all things through Christ who strengthens me."

Prayer:

Dearest Lord, I know that You can do everything, and that no thought can be hidden from You. You have given me the assurance in Your words that You will bolster my spirit once I trust in You so that I will be able to shift my mind and attitude to recognize that I am capable, competent and worthy. Help me, Lord, to soar above the storms of life knowing that You will keep me elevated and will equip me for Your use and purpose. Amen!

Day 11

Rely Completely On God

Affirmation

I rely on God completely because I know that in Him there is peace, power and prosperity. I can, therefore, release any feelings of inadequacy, incompetence and unworthiness that lingers within me.

> *My voice shall thou hear in the morning, O Lord; in the morning will I direct my prayer unto thee, and will look up. (Psalms 5:3).*

Scientists establish that we need at least four basic elements for survival: air, water, food and light. This is indisputable because they are all essential to our existence. We simply cannot live without any of these fundamentals.

Interestingly, the Word of God proclaims and confirms that Jesus is air, water, food and light:

- **Jesus is the breath of life:** *The spirit of God hath made me, and the breath of the Almighty hath given me life. (Job 33:4).*

- **Jesus is the source of living water:** *He that believeth on me, as the scripture hath said, out of his belly shall flow rivers of living water. (John 7:38).*

- **Jesus is the Bread of life:** *I am the living bread which came from heaven: if any man eat of this bread, he shall live forever: and the bread that I will give is my flesh, which I will give for the life of the world. (John 6:51).*

- **Jesus is the light of the world:** *I am the light of the world: he that followeth me shall not walk in darkness, but shall have the light of life. (John 8:12b).*

Science has essentially confirmed that we cannot live without Jesus, as He is a combination of the four most significant elements that are necessary for survival.

We breathe, eat, live and are sustained exclusively through Christ. Therefore, man's opinion of us doesn't and cannot preserve us. We should never give anyone the power or authority to dictate our worth and value. It is in Christ that we have complete reliance and in Him we truly subsist. His opinion of us is what truly matters.

Those who fail to trust in and rely on Him are not truly living a wholesome life. They have a vacuum and void within that prevents them from truly living a flourishing and fulfilled life and, ultimately, their existence is fated to imminent doom.

> *Though a sinner do evil an hundred times, and his days be prolonged, yet surely I know that it shall be well with them that fear God, which fear before him. But it shall not be well with the wicked, neither shall he prolong his days, which are as a shadow; because he feareth not before God. (Ecclesiastes 8:12-13).*

Notwithstanding this caution, God doesn't desire for us to rely on Him out of a spirit of fear but out of love, knowing that He cares for us and wants us to live a life of confidence and boldness. He wants to elevate us where we have been relegated.

Complete reliance means that we submit our incompetence in the presence of His omnipotence. We submit our powerlessness and behold His awesomeness. We submit our inadequacy and rely on His supremacy.

It is through this submission and reliance that He will transform our incompetence into proficiency, our limitations to authority and our inadequacy to sufficiency.

> *I am the vine, ye are the branches: He that abideth in me, and I in him, the same bringeth forth much fruit: for without me ye can do nothing. (John 15:5).*

So when you are tempted to give in to feelings of self-doubt, insufficiency, inadequacy, rejection and self-pity, as a result of others response and treatment of you, rely on the One who "...*raiseth up the poor out of the dust, and lifteth up the needy out of the dunghill. (Psalm 113:7).*

Being confident of this very thing, that he which hath begun a good work in you will perform it until the day of Jesus Christ. (Philippians 1:6).

I, therefore, challenge you to rely on God and watch Him transform your life completely.

Eagle Instinct: Relying on God means that we trust Him in all seasons. In good times and bad, in highs and lows, with the assurance that He knows what is always best for us.

The eagle masters what is called "change management." Whenever she is about to lay her eggs, she and her mate makes the nest comfortable and homely, finding and using the softest and best materials to cushion it. However, when she believes that her eaglet is ready for flight, she begins removing the padding that she used for her eaglet's comfort. She allows the sticks and brambles to scratch her little one sometimes causing serious bleeding. For many looking on, this is deemed as a cruel act, but it is in this process that the eaglet starts to flap its wings and starts developing strength in her wings in order to gain the required muscle and confidence to fly.

When we rely on God, we must trust Him in both the favorable and unfavorable periods of our lives. There are times when He will pad our nests and make life comfortable and cozy, while in other times He will remove these comforting materials that layer our nest and leave us bare and susceptible to the thorns and prickles of life. This action may cause us to bleed emotionally, shed gallons of tears and leave us sore but He doesn't do this because He doesn't love us; in fact, He does this because He loves us and wants us to take our flight. It is in the challenging moments in life we are tried and gain the strength to prove our competency, adequacy, worthiness and develop spinal tenacity and intestinal fortitude. More so, if our nest didn't become uncomfortable, we would not learn to fly.

Therefore, as He sees it fit, He will line your nests or leave you bare. If He leaves you bare, know that He is strengthening you for flight and elevation.

Prayer:

Lord, I rely on You wholeheartedly because I know that it is in You that I will be strengthened to deal with the challenges of life. I am not always assertive and assured of my calling and purpose as I ought to. Sometimes the cares of life become overwhelming and burdensome but I know that once I rely on You, You will deliver and bless me immeasurably. Teach me to be faithful and true in all that I do. Amen

Day 12

Glorify God With Your Gifts

Affirmation

I am gifted and endowed with an immeasurable distribution of talents and competences. I will use them to bless the lives of others and glorify God.

As every man hath received the gift, even so minister the same one to another, as good stewards of the manifold grace of God. (1 Peter 4:10).

Many dreams and gifts have been aborted because of the affliction of unworthiness. Millions of people go to their graves without discovering or fully embracing the gifts they were created with.

Les Brown, an icon of modern day motivation, express that, "The graveyard is the richest place on earth because it is here that you will find all the hopes and dreams that were never fulfilled, the books that were never written, the songs that were never sang, the inventions that were never shared, the cures that were never discovered, all because someone was too afraid to take the first step, keep with the problem to carry out their dreams."

If I might add to this profound testimonial, many dreams also died because persons allowed the opinions of others to sway, diminish their dreams and lead them to feel unworthy.

History and the salvation story, as we know it, would not be the same if the great great great great grandmother of Jesus had not acknowledged and used her gifts at a critical juncture. She probably didn't consider how critical a role her gifts played in advancing the kingdom and glorifying God, but she certainly hit a home run with what she did.

She could have proffered countless excuses expressing unworthiness, but Rahab did not allow the skeletons in her closet or the labels society placed on her to prevent her from using her wit and brilliance to assist the Israelites in entering Canaan. She boldly and brilliantly used her adept negotiation abilities to save both the Israelite spies and her entire family. She did not allow the dark cloud of her profession as a prostitute to prevent her from asserting her abilities and fulfilling her purpose.

Therefore, you should not allow the obscurity of your past, the mistakes you have made or people's opinion of you to prevent you from shining your effervescent light. Countless people are depending on your gifts to comfort, enlighten and bring them closer to God.

> *Let your light so shine before men, that they may see your good work and glorify your Father which is in heaven. (Matthew 5:16).*

When we refuse to spread our wings or shine our lights, we advance the kingdom of the enemy. However, when we make the determination to grow where we are planted and to make good use of our endowments, comes what may, we bring honor to our sovereign God who has lavished us with His excellent gifts.

Every good gift and every perfect gift is from above, and cometh down from the Father of lights, with whom is no variableness, neither shadow of turning. (James 1:17).

Never diminish your abilities or compare your gift with others. What is inside you is of an immeasurable value and could influence the course of time.

Embrace every opportunity and stand firm in your worthiness knowing that you have only one lifetime to live out your purpose. Therefore, *"Whatsoever thy hand findeth to do, do it with thy might; for there is no work nor device, nor knowledge, nor wisdom, in the grave, wither thou goest." (Ecclesiastes 9:10).*

When we release and liberate ourselves by making a radical shift, relying completely on God and glorifying Him with our gifts, it doesn't matter what is lurking in our past, or how we are regarded by our fellow man; we will walk fully in our calling, embrace our PURPOSE and, in so doing, make a sound investment in our current life and hereafter.

And let us not be weary in well doing: for in due season we shall reap, if we faint not. (Galatians 6:9).

Eagle Instinct: One of the most referenced and admired ability of the eagle is its strong vision. An eagle can see four to five times better than a human being. They can see five basic colors compared to our three. They can detect UV light. An eagle is extremely focused and can see its enemy from afar. It is extremely swift, meticulous and calculated and uses these attributes to protect its young and to pick up things far in the distance.

For example, when the snake attacks the nest to steal the eggs or kill her young, the eagle can pick this up from miles away and swiftly fly to the rescue of her young.

We are all endowed with various gifts and talents to protect, empower and bless others. Nia activated her protection instinct, but it wasn't appreciated. In the same manner, use your protective instinct to assist others. If you encounter opposition or ingratitude, the Bible tells us to do good anyway as we glorify God with our gifts.

Like the eagle, we all have the ability to be visionaries. We all possess the ability to think, process, make critical choices, plan for the future and use our gifts to enhance the lives around us and advance God's kingdom.

Where there is no vision, the people perish. (Proverbs 29:18a).

I challenge you to block out every form of distraction and activate your eagle instinct by focusing and devising a plan on how you can use your gifts, small or great, to bless others, glorify God and to keep your eyes focus on Christ.

Prayer:

Precious Lord, I thank You for the many gifts You have entrusted me with. Like the precious eggs of an eagle, the serpent is always devising to steal and destroy them. I pray that You protect and shield my gifts and give me the will to boldly assert them. May I never misuse and abuse my gifts but use them to glorify and enhance Your Kingdom. Amen.

Chapter 5

To Feel Burdened With Guilt, Shame And Stagnation

At some point in our lives we have carried some baggage of some sort. Two of the heaviest articles in our bags that can weigh us down for a very long time and leave us stagnated are guilt and shame.

When guilt and shame are tenants in the apartment of your brain, they can create such damage and mess that you may not be able to recognize yourself during or after their tenancy. They are two sloppy and overweight freeloaders who sit around and feed on all your productive energy and leave you feeling drained and useless. These guys held Nia hostage. She felt guilty for being awesome. She worried about offending those around her and was riddled with shame for being different.

Believe it or not, many persons are struck with this same virus. Their environment and the people around them limit, strangle and suffocate their potentials by working on their psychology. Subconsciously, this is what Nia's siblings did. They just couldn't handle her enormous character. Everything she did was offensive to them and they managed to convince her that she was deficient rather than proficient. Not only was she holding back but she was ashamed and guilty for being the way she was.

So it is that some persons are afraid to dream big because it will offend those around them. Some are afraid of speaking because persons laugh at them and brutally criticize their tone, range, accent, fluency and pitch. Some people refuse to display their talents because they are deemed as showing off.

Today I want to encourage you to:

1. Unpack your baggage.
2. Break the chains holding you back.
3. Be still.

Day 13

Unpack Your Baggage

Affirmation

I will unpack and release my burden of guilt and shame which holds me captive and allow God to perfume my soul with His wonderful grace and manifold favor.

Cast thy burden upon the Lord, and he shall sustain thee: he shall not suffer the righteous to be moved. (Psalm 55:22).

You may have heard the saying, "Hurt people hurt people." Many people go around hemorrhaging on other persons who had nothing to do with the initial hurt inflicted on them. Then those they hurt end up hurting other people and the cycle continues endemically.

Many persons were raised by ailing parents who were psychologically and mentally scarred, who ended up scarring them subconsciously. They, in-turn, carry this childhood baggage from their cradle to the casket. It is like a ruptured cyst bleeding on every soul that crosses their path and preventing them from growing and thriving.

This oversized cyst holds their past hurts, pains, sorrows, ill-feelings, bitterness and scars from betrayal, rejection, back-stabs, neglect, abuse and a host of other troubles.

The Scripture tell us about a woman who was carrying a burden for twelve long years. She was ostracized and scorned by everyone. She must have felt sorrowful, lonely and ashamed by this malady that no medical expert or home remedy could cure. She desired desperately to be free and get absolute healing from this affliction so that she could live a prosperous and fulfilling life. Her life was one of shame, guilt and stagnation.

The beauty about her story is that she knew that something was wrong with her. She acknowledged that she was ailing, and she was determined to find healing. Her story is one of the most intriguing stories of faith recorded in the Bible. It must take a lot of faith for someone to press into a crowd un-chaperoned, going against the strict regulations and conventions of her culture, just to touch the hem of the Savior's garment. Her act was one wrought with desperation, determination and dedication and this is how she secured her healing. The healing was not in the hem, but in her hard-pressed faith.

> *But Jesus turned him about, and when he saw her, he said, Daughter, be of good comfort; thy faith had made thee whole. And the woman was made whole from this hour. (Matthew 9:22).*

Are you desperate enough? Determined enough? Dedicated enough?

This story is a very inspiring and prescriptive one. It is time to unpack the baggage by reaching out in faith and touching the hem of Jesus' garment. The story of this fascinating miracle may have spread abroad and inspired others back then because later in Matthew 14 we learn in verse 35 and 36 that, "...*when the men of that place had knowledge of him, they sent out into all that country round about, and brought unto him all that were diseased; And besought him that they might only touch the hem of his garment: and as many as touched were made perfectly whole.*"

These too were desperate, determined and dedicated. Today, touching His hem requires some form of unloading. The baggage you are carrying is preventing you from pressing through and making that faith touch.

I want to encourage you today to unpack that baggage you have been carrying. Knock off the locks and start releasing. It is certainly not the will of the Lord that you should be pressed and crushed with undue burdens. There is no need for you to carry shame and guilt around when Jesus died on the cross and paid the penalty. He did so that you could be free; that you could live out your purpose and live a productive and fulfilling life. Nothing or no-one has the power to deprive you of this privilege.

Jesus' prerogative is to relieve you of your heavy burden of guilt and feelings of hopelessness. He invites you to, *"Come unto me, all ye that labor and are heavy laden, and I will give you rest. Take my yoke upon you, and learn of me; for I am meek and lowly in heart: and ye shall find rest unto your souls. For my yoke is easy, and my burden is light." (Matthew 11:28-30).*

He calls us to humbly seek Him and lay all our burdens at His feet.

> *Humble yourselves under the mighty hand of God, that he may exalt you in due time: Casting all your care upon Him; for he careth for you. (1 Peter 5:6-7).*

No matter your age or the stage of your cyst; no matter how long you have been bleeding or had your baggage of guilt, shame and stagnation packed, it is time to unpack and let go so that you can soar. God promised to relieve and take care of you, even when you become old and gray.

> *And even to your old age I am he; and even to hoar hairs I will carry you: I have made, and I will bear; even I will carry, and will deliver you. (Isaiah 46:4).*

Therefore, let this be your declaration today:

> *Behold, God is my salvation; I will trust, and not be afraid: for the Lord JEHOVAH is my strength*

and my song; he also is become my salvation. (Isaiah 12:2).

Eagle Instinct: The eagle is known to be the strongest of the bird species. However, like everything that flies, they are governed by aerodynamics. Experts have noted that the wings support both the weight of the eagle, which ranges between 8-12 pounds, as well as its cargo. Eagles seldom fly with anything more than half of their body weight. Hence, their lifting power is estimated at four or five pounds.

Naturally, the eagle uses its strength to take food items to its nest to feed its eaglets. Ordinarily, they do not fly around, glide or soar with weights. That is physically impossible.

Therefore, while we may have to carry some sort of baggage at different points in our lives, it should be on a temporary basis and it should not be overweighed. You should then unpack and unload the baggage you are carrying constantly so you can "mount up with wings" and glide through life unencumbered like the eagle.

Prayer:

In Thee, O Lord, do I put my trust; let me never be ashamed: deliver me in thy righteousness. Infill me with Your transforming powers and strengthen me so that I will reach out and touch the hem of Your garment by faith. Remove the locks from the baggage I am carrying. Deliver and direct me as I unpack the hurt, sorrows, pain, scars, grief and turmoil that are stagnating my growth and weighing me down with guilt and shame so that my wings will be free and light for flight. Consecrate me and relieve me of my burden. Amen.

Day 14

Break The Chains Holding You Back

Affirmation

I serve a God who is capable and eager to break the chains that hold me captive. I will yield to His will so that my chains of shame, guilt and stagnation will be broken.

> *Stand fast therefore in the liberty wherewith Christ hath made us free, and not be entangled again with the yoke of bondage. (Galatians 5:1).*

In Luke 8 we learn of a demoniac who was fettered in chains. He was in the most debase state a human being could find himself. Torn and ravaged by sin and legions of demons that tormented his soul night and day, he languished in pain and roamed the cemetery for years, it would appear, until he was found and delivered by the Savior. Not only did he find companionship with the dead, but he spent his days cutting himself and screeching in share horror as his life degenerated.

This condition is indisputably one of the most extreme and horrific that a human being could find him or herself. However, many of us are fettered in spiritual chains. We

88

may not appear to be tattered, torn, wild and non-coherent as the demoniac, but we are shackled and chained by the circumstances of our lives.

Some of us spend our days in the burial ground of negative and destructive thinking, screeching internally from the pains of guilt, hurt and regret and occasionally assassinating our own characters with critical and self-mutilating thoughts. Many of us are plagued with demons of self-doubt, anger, bitterness, grief, depression and a host of other destructive afflictions. There are different levels and stages to this burdensome infirmity. Some are milder than others, but many of us are chained and shackled by varied circumstances that need to be broken for us to live a truly satisfying and wholesome life.

When this suffering soul saw the Savior, He fell in front of Him and cried out. Demons tremble in the presence of the Lord! Therefore, we should seek the Lord diligently so that we can have peace, joy, and freedom.

> *But seek ye first the kingdom of God, and his righteousness; and all these things shall be added unto you. (Matthew 6:33).*

> *The Lord is good unto them that wait for him, to the soul that seeketh Him. (Lamentations 3:25).*

You may be imprisoned and held captive by the shame and guilt that you carry daily. You remain stagnated because you are incarcerated by the burdens you bear. Sometimes it is so intense that you cannot seem to find the strength to reach out to God. In these circumstances you need others to petition on your behalf. You need friends and loved ones to lift you up. When Peter was imprisoned, he was lifted in prayer by his church family.

> *Peter therefore was kept in prison: but prayer was made without ceasing of the Church unto God for him. (Acts 12:5).*

This prayer festival impressed upon the heavenly throng favorably and moved the Lord to respond in a marvelous manner.

> *And when Herod would have brought him forth, the same night Peter was sleeping between two soldiers, bound with two chains: and the keepers before the door kept the prison. And, behold, the angel of the Lord came upon him, and a light shined in the prison: and he smote Peter on the side, and raised him up, saying, Arise up quickly. And his chains fell off from his hands. (Acts 12:6-7).*

God still works incredible miracles like these, and He yearns to work them in your life. He can release you in the most miraculous and amazing way.

Peter's situation was not the only of its kind documented in the Bible. Paul and Silas were in a similar position, locked up in a prison cell. They prayed and lifted up praises unto God.

And suddenly there was a great earthquake, so that the foundations of the prison were shaken: and immediately all the doors were opened, and everyone's bands were loosed. (Acts 16:26).

Consequently, the chains and shackles that hold you captive can be broken when:

1. You fall prostrate at the Savior's feet, like the demoniac of Gadarene, and have Jesus cast out the demons that plague your soul.

2. When you invite and ask your tribe, community of faith or companions to pray for you, like Peter, He will dispatch angels to shine His light on you and free you from your chains.

3. When you pray and shout praises unto God, like Paul and Silas, He will send a great quake in your life to shake and break the circumstantial chains that hold you captive, open doors and set you free.

I challenge you today to cry out to God and let Him bring you out of darkness and break the chains that hold you captive, as He did for so many others:

Then they cried unto the Lord in their trouble, and he saved them out of their distresses. He brought them out of darkness and the shadow of death, and brake their bands in sunder. (Psalm 107:13-14).

Eagle Instinct: Eagles do not associate with other species of birds. Eagles fly only with eagles!

The unfortunate circumstance that Nia was thrust in is the root to all her evils and dilemma. She was surrounded by the wrong people. She had no choice in the matter as, usually, eagles never hang around or associate with other species of birds. Their standards are superbly high, and they really cannot relate to other birds.

Like Nia, we endure much distress and feelings of captivity and imprisonment because of the people we associate with. We should have friends and associates who can lift us up in prayer, petition earnestly on our behalf and give praise and adulation to God with us. Our circle, and the people we entrust our secrets to, should be people of like minds who can help to build and strengthen our faith-wings.

Therefore, in activating our Eagle Instinct, we need to do a thorough check of our inner circle. Am I surrounded by chickens or eagles? Are my friends and associates dependable and loyal? Are they encouraging and supporting my walk with God? Be mindful that, *"He that walketh with wise men shall be wise: but a companion of fools shall be destroyed." (Proverbs 13:20).*

Prayer:

O Lord, truly I am Thy servant: Thou hast loosed my bonds. You have heard my hearts plea and I know You will deliver and break the shackles of shame, guilt and stagnation that holds me captive. Deliver me from associations that may be contributing to my captivity. I fall at Your feet knowing that You have never resisted the soul that seek and clings to You. I glorify You and sing praises to Your name for what You are about to wrought in my life. Bless my friends and associates and deliver them as well. Thank You for Your continued grace and mercy. Amen.

Day 15

Be Still

Affirmation

I know that the Lord will deliver me from all forms of shame and guilt. I will therefore 'Be still' and allow Him to have His perfect way.

Be still, and know that I am God. (Psalm 46:10a).

If you are an avid movie fanatic, you may observe in scores of Hollywood films and movies that the idea of standing or being still in impending danger is extensively explored. The idea is that if you stay still, you stand a high chance of escaping and eluding whatever danger looms. This standing still phenomena is utilized to evoke much intrigue and builds the momentum in any drama piece.

Whether it is a snake, a wild animal, a predator, the antagonist, or whoever it may be, playwrights and film creators play on the "be still" premise and heighten levels of anticipation, mystery and, sometimes, sheer terror and dread through their sound manipulation. This tool is used as a control and sometimes mild hypnosis that induces a series of heightened emotions ranging from fear to trepidation, sometimes causing the spectator to feel as if they are the ones placed in the precarious position.

God gives us a command to "be still," not to manipulate or cause our hearts to flutter and panic in apprehension; not so we can lie low and escape whatever danger may be looming, but for the incredible purpose of calming and soothing us through the assurance that He has us covered. He wants us to "be still" and know that He will deliver, redeem, bless and establish us.

All of us have encountered some manner of storm in our lives. Jesus' "be still" command is for the purpose of silencing the howling winds of fear, calming the treacherous waves of hurt, halting the fierce hails of guilt and resting the frightening thunders of gloom and despair.

Jesus and His disciples, in the gospel of Mark, encountered a literal storm that caused the disciples to panic in fear of perishing. While the disciples were all on deck bailing the water from the ship and making every effort to prevent the ship from sinking, Jesus was below deck, in the belly of the ship, sleeping peacefully as if oblivious to the storm that was wreaking havoc in and around the ship. It was not until the disciples went in search and sought for Him that, "*...He arose, and rebuked the wind, and said unto the sea, Peace, be still. And the wind cease, and there was a great calm." (Mark 4:39).*

Jesus wants to pronounce this calm and peace in our lives in the same manner. It is not His desire that we should be battered, torn, worn and tossed about by the storms of life. It is not His desire for us to hyperventilate and run around in sheer alarm and, possibly, lose our sanity. He doesn't want us to languish hopeless in shame and guilt. He wants you to know that, *"The Lord shall fight for you, and ye shall hold your peace." (Exodus 14:14).* There are three lessons we can learn from this situation:

1. Fear and panic will not help any situation. What is required is FAITH. The disciples were clearly distressed amidst the tempest and turmoil. They got themselves excessively worked up and distraught by what was happening. When they called on Jesus, He responded immediately and rebuked the storm then asked them, *"Why are ye so fearful? How is it that ye have no faith?" (Mark 4:40b).*

2. Jesus is waiting on us to seek after Him and invite Him to work on our behalf. Jesus knew the catastrophic events that were playing out above deck. Yet, He stayed put in His reverie and waited on them to call on Him. We have to wake Jesus up in our lives and invite Him to calm our storms. He desires for us to trust and depend on Him to work on our behalf.

   Seek the Lord while he may be found, call ye upon him when he is near. (Isaiah 55:6).

3. Jesus wants us to emulate Him and "be still." Jesus was "still" despite nature's eruption. He chose to rest in that very moment. There is no other human act that fully captures the essence of "stillness" like sleep. Jesus' action is a vivid illustration of how God wants us to feel when we are in a storm. We should not lose sleep when the storms of life are raging. Jesus wants you to, *"Be still, and know that I am God." (Psalm 46:10a).*

He invites us to find peace in His words; to feed on the life-giving power that comes from them and learn to trust and heed His commands. He also desires for us to learn to be still, *"...and ...study to be quiet..." (See 1 Thessalonians 4:11).*

When we come to know God and make all effort to "be still," we allow Him to have His perfect way. He will then reward us with peace and contentment. Shame, guilt and stagnation will have no place or lot with us. Righteousness will have His way:

> *And the work of righteousness shall be peace; and the effect of righteousness quietness and assurance for ever. (Isaiah 32:17).*

I challenge you today to try standing still; to shift your mind, look up and invite God to calm the storms in your life without getting alarmed and panicked. This is certainly a step of Christian maturity where you can declare:

Surely I have behaved and quieted myself, as a child that is weaned of his mother: my soul is even as a weaned child. (Psalm 131:2).

Eagle Instinct: If you want to know the power of being still, the eagle is one of the most profound creation acts to observe and emulate in this regard. The eagle will stay perched for hours, scanning the horizon and the ground, taking in everything that is going on while making calculated decisions to pounce on a prey or to shield her nest. She calmly stays in one position as if listening to the wind before taking off in a calculated manner, with a purpose and aim in mind. The eagle doesn't fly around and flitter without purpose.

Like the eagle, we ought to learn to master the art of being still. It is in these moments that we hear the voice of God as He speaks to us. We need to quiet the noise in our heads and still our fluttering nerves. We need to allow the Lord to instruct us and give us the answers to our queries and concerns so that we can take off with a purpose, aim and determination.

Prayer:

Lord, I desire to "be still." I want to be able to hear when You speak to my soul and calm the tempests in my life. You commanded the raging storm to be still and it obeyed. I invite You now to command my spirit to be still so that You can perform whatever surgery or operations needed to uproot shame and guilt from my life. I trust

You to calm and soothe my soul with Your words and Your touch. Deliver and bless me now. Amen.

Chapter 6

To Wait, Suffer Long And Constantly Desire More

We spend our lives waiting; waiting for nine months to make our appearance in this world; waiting to grow enough muscle strength and agility to walk; waiting to have our teeth pop up out of our gums, to have them set loose and fall out to wait again for them to re-grow.

We wait for every birthday to come to grow older and develop. We wait long to become teenagers then adults. We wait in lines to catch buses and other transportation, to see the doctor, to do exams and interviews. We wait to be served food in restaurants and to have our groceries purchased in stores and supermarkets. We wait to marry, grow old and eventually die.

We wait all our lives and through it, we are bound to experience some sort of suffering, ill-fate, loss and turmoil of different variations and degrees, some more than others.

We are always seeking and searching and desiring and working towards a higher goal, a greater calling. It is in our very nature.

We saw Nia, watching. The script didn't mention her waiting but, without even giving it much deliberation, she was. We are always waiting to see what will happen next and, naturally, she would be hoping and desiring for better. We usually do when we are uncomfortable or during some distress.

So it is, we are always waiting and desiring for better and, at times, we get tired of waiting, suffering long and desiring more. I want to assure you that there is more! Defeat, destitution and despondence is not your destination. You can have better. You just need to:

1. Wait in the Lord.
2. Delight in the Lord.
3. Trust and obey.

Day 16

Wait In The Lord

Affirmation

I will wait on and in the Lord while doing His will and allow Him to have His true and perfect way in my life so that He will renew my strength.

> *But they that wait upon the Lord shall renew their strength; they shall mount up with wings as eagles; they shall run, and not be weary; and they shall walk, and not faith. (Isaiah 40:31).*

No, the caption is not a typographical error! The Bible tells us to wait on the Lord, but today I dare to stretch the command a bit and invite you to "wait in the Lord" as you "wait on the Lord."

History has revealed countless stories of persons who gave up after waiting or made rash decisions in the interim because they got frustrated, exhausted, lost hope or caved under the pressure they encountered while waiting.

What makes the difference during the wait is complete reliance, rest and TRUST that Abba Father's plans are perfect and that the wait is necessary.

Rest in the Lord, and wait patiently for him. (Psalm 37:7a).

I remember, as a child, breaking tropical almonds with stones to extract the delectable nut inside. It was a very dangerous activity that we thought was worth the prize. I remember beating the dried and sometimes green shells for what seemed like hours with my cousins to get to the paradise within. At times, after getting frustrated, we collectively picked up a huge boulder and drop it on the nuts and, often, the almond would squash under the pressure and was pretty useless to us then. This is what happens when we lose patience and fail to wait in the Lord while waiting on Him; we squash our dreams and abort the plans He has for us when we run ahead or try to birth our dreams on our own, prematurely.

Abraham waited on the Lord but did not wait in Him. What's the difference? When we just wait on the Lord, we leave ourselves exposed to the enemy whose prerogative is to frustrate and distract us. It is like driving without insurance coverage. Yes, we are driving, but in the face of adversity or calamity we have no assurance or indemnity; we are easily compromised and susceptible to a loss.

However, when we wait in Him, we have full coverage and assurance that, comes what may, we will be compensated. We see no option or possibility than the one He ordains. We do not proffer possible solutions or alternatives and our faith is heavily rooted and grounded to the point that our thoughts, words and actions exude complete trust in His will and promise. We will not be lured or influenced to give into external counsel. Abraham allowed His wife to sway his faith and focus while they waited on the promised child and the outcome was a shattered almond; a birth of a nation, the descendants of Ishmael, which are the Arabs, that have been wreaking havoc for centuries in the Middle East and on Christianity. So it is when we are waiting on the Lord and are not fully immersed and trusting in Him. We could end up courting doubt, losing our focus, veering off course and giving birth to disaster.

Hannah was a perfect example of what it means to "wait in the Lord." She couldn't just wait on the Lord because God did not promise her a child. She was biologically compromised. She was barren because the Lord had shut up her womb. If she had just sat in wait, hopeless and given to depression, and did not fortify her wait with supplication, she would not have impressed God to move in her favor and perform a miracle. She earnestly sought and beseeched the Lord to move on her behalf.

Some of the things we desire for God to do on our behalf requires supernatural power. Waiting on God sometimes is just not enough. We must wait in Him through Prayer, Pleading and Praise. Some things require a higher degree of supplication through earnest fasting and prayer.

And He said unto them, this kind can come forth by nothing, but by prayer and fasting. (Mark 9:29).

I, therefore, advance the thought that waiting on the Lord is not enough. You also have to "wait in Him" so that He can work on your behalf and give you what you desire most, declaring, *"My soul, wait thou only upon God; for my expectation is from him."(Psalm 62:5).*

While you wait, ask God to order your thoughts, words, deeds and steps. Ask Him to prepare you, to mold and fashion you in His perfect image.

Teach me, and I will hold my tongue: and cause me to understand wherein I have erred. (Job 6:24).

Eagle Instinct: Eagles are monogamous. They generally date one mate for their entire life. They both depend on each other and work together in providing for, nurturing and protecting their eggs and young ones. They even take turns sitting on their eggs to have them incubated. They learn to wait, trust and depend on each other.

So it is that God desires for us to put all our trust in Him. He desires for us to be monogamous and practice worship fidelity. What is taking our attention? What are we giving our trust, attention and affection? In the same manner that the eagles stick to each other for life, support and care for their mates, so it is that God wants to be the love of our soul, to protect us, care and provide for us.

Therefore, as the eagle waits on her mate, never doubting that he will stick by her, so it is the Lord wants us to have that trust in Him and to wait in Him as we wait on Him.

Prayer:

Truly my soul wait on the Lord: from Him cometh my salvation. I not only wait on You, mighty God, but I wait in You. I wait, clinging desperately on Your promises and I bare my soul completely to You. Please accept my sacrifice of praise as I fall prostrate at Your feet casting all my cares upon You. Hear and answer my cry as You wrap, tie and tangle me in Your awesome will. Amen.

Day 17

Delight In The Lord

Affirmation

I will delight in the Lord who has called and ordained me, knowing that even though I may wait and suffer long, because I trust in Him and do His will, He will give me what my heart desires.

Delight also in the Lord: and he shall give thee the desires of thine heart. (Psalm 37:4).

There is nothing the Lord finds more delightful that when His crowned creation, the "apple of his eye," the beneficiary of His manifold favor, delights in Him. He has fashioned and designed some amazing wonders within and beyond the earth in the other worlds, but none of His created work gratifies and thrills the Almighty like the marvelous subject of His love and adoration, created in His very image: human beings.

He delighteth not in the strength of the horse: he taketh not pleasure in the legs of a man. The Lord taketh pleasure in them that fear him, in them that hope in his mercy. (Psalm 147:10-11).

A mother is thrilled and derives the most blissful and pleasurable feeling when the child that comes from her womb excels and showers her with positive reception and appreciation. A lover, too, is most delighted when the love that they radiate and lavish on the recipient of their affection is reciprocated.

Consequently, God is that mother Eagle who "...*stirreth up her nest, fluttereth over her young, spreadeth abroad her wings, taketh them, beareth them on her wings.*" *(Deuteronomy 32:11).* He provides, protects, sustains, builds, chastens and comforts because He loves and cares for us. Jehovah Jireh delights in providing for His children. He is the God who declares that, "...*no good thing will he withhold from them that walk uprightly.*" *(Proverbs 84:11b).* He is the God who made the ultimate sacrifice and laid down His life for us. All that He asks and requires is that we do His will and delight in Him.

> *For the Lord taketh pleasure in his people: he will beautify the meek with salvation. (Psalm 149:4).*

No matter what this life throws at us, there is always something to delight in God about. The very fact that you are reading this devotional is something to rejoice over. Sadly, we allow the cares of this life to overwhelm and shroud our minds so much that we fail to see and recognize how much God does for us on an hourly, minutely and per second basis.

Because we have suffered much, waited long and sometimes grown weary, we forget to acknowledge and identify the blessings in and around us. The key in delighting in the Lord is to activate a pulse of gratitude; to find a reason to give God thanks; to appreciate Him for all that He does for us.

- Some persons have strained family relationships and find it difficult to tolerate some of their family members. While asking God to work on the family and bring unity and love, thank Him for giving you a family. Someone somewhere is wishing they had at least one known or living family member.

- Some persons have a job that is draining and causing them distress. While asking God to provide a new job or a better source of income, thank God you have a job and a means of subsistence. Some people are desirous of and are praying desperately for a job.

- Some persons have children who give them headaches and heartaches. While asking God to work on them and make them better, thank Him for giving you children. Countless women around the world are in grave sorrow, languishing and crying their hearts out wishing, more than anything, that they could have at least one child.

- Some persons have a life they believe sucks. They are troubled and afflicted with various problems. While asking God to fix these issues and bring deliverance, thank Him for a life. Many persons lost their lives without getting the chance to live out their purpose, while others are on borrowed time because of terminal illness.

We complain about our appearance, abilities, the food we eat, wants, associates, homes, car and community, without giving much thought to the blessings and favor that hovers over our lives. God is inviting us to count our blessings, to identify the great things He is doing for us and to delight in Him.

God is calling for us first to understand Him: *Acquaint now thyself with him, and be at peace: thereby good will come unto thee. For then shalt thou have thy delight in the Almighty, and shalt lift up thy face unto God. (Job 22:21 & 26).*

God is calling for us to taste and see that He is good: *I sat down under his shadow with great delight, and his fruit was sweet to my taste. (Song of Solomon 2:3b).*

God is calling for us to forsake our evil ways and any form of company or association that will corrupt or lead us away from Him: *Blessed is the man that walketh not in the counsel of the ungodly, nor standeth in the way of sinners, nor sitteth in the way of the scornful. (Psalm 1:1).*

God is calling us to delight in His word and take heed to the counsels in it: *Thy testimonies are also my delight and my counselors. (Psalm 119:24).*

God is calling us to delight in His commandment and His statutes: *But his delight is in the law of the Lord; and in his law doth he meditate day and night. (Psalm 1:2). Make me to go in the path of thy commandments; for therein do I delight. (Psalms 119:35).*

God is calling us to praise Him: *Praise ye the Lord. Blessed is the man that feareth the Lord, that delight greatly in his commandments. (Psalm 112:1).*

I challenge you today: No matter how bleak or dismal your situation may seem to be; no matter how long you have been waiting or suffering with one or more afflictions, find at least three things to give God thanks for. Delight in Him and watch Him work marvelously in your life.

Eagle Instinct: An eagle is what is called an apex predator or top or alpha predators. This means that they are at the top of the food chain with no natural predator. They are carnivorous and live on a diet of meat and fish. They eat whatever animal is available to them. They do not consume dead meat, which is meat or flesh of animals that died naturally or are killed and left by another animal. An apex predator, in the animal kingdom, denotes greatness and supremacy as they are not threatened by any other species. These animals were given such worthy

111

statuses because the Lord delights in them as they help in balancing the eco-system and exude His power.

Human beings were given more authority and power to have dominion even over these great species. This, therefore, makes us indisputably greater as we are God's most prized work of creation.

Many commentators liken the fresh, meat-eating tendency of the eagle to the practice of refraining from gossiping. Gossiping is said to be like scavenging or feeding on dead meat. Gossiping is not a practice that is acceptable for a child of God. It contradicts the idea of delighting in the Lord. Therefore, when we delight in the Lord, we speak of His wonderful acts; we focus on His goodness; we maintain a positive and productive mind and conduct ourselves like an apex or alpha predator, rather than a weak prey.

The eagle delights in the Lord as she spreads her wings and glides in all her grandeur through the sky. God also desires for us to glide, soar and delight in Him and, as His marvelous work of creation, live up to our true potential and allow Him to have His perfect way through and with us.

Prayer:

Holy God, my soul longs to delight in You. I am longing to feel Your healing and comforting touch. I know no evil or forms of shadow can cohabitate with Your light and presence because Your holiness is like a consuming fire. Please take full control and authority as I show gratitude and appreciation for what You have done and intend to do with, for and through me. Keep me true and wholly depending on You. Amen.

Day 18

Trust And Obey

Affirmation

I trust and make a daily commitment to obey the will of the Lord, knowing that He will bless, establish and reward my obedience.

> *The Lord recompense thy work, and a full reward be given thee of the Lord God of Israel, under whose wings thou art come to trust. (Ruth 2:12).*

Trust is one of the most integral ingredients in a relationship. A relationship devoid of trust is pointless, counter-productive and dysfunctional. According to Stephen Covey, American Educator and keynote speaker, "Trust is the glue of life. It's the most essential ingredient in effective communication. It's the foundational principle that holds all relationships."

Trust was instituted by God and it is the essence of the harmonious idyllic connection He desires for us to have with Him. He wants us to recognize that He is faithful and just and that He "...*is not slack concerning his promise, as some men count slackness, but is longsuffering to us-*

114

ward, not willing that any should perish but that all should come to repentance."(2 Peter 3:9).

He is a perfect God. His ways, words and principles are faultless and for our best interest. Anything that He professes He possesses and will bring to past. He is proven to be powerful, prolific, pardoning and precise with bringing to pass His promises. Men fail, gives false hope, mislead and disappoint but *"As for God, his way is perfect; the word of the Lord is tried: he is a buckler to all them that trust in him." (2 Samuel 22:31).*

Noah trusted God and was spared from imminent doom because, even though the command he received to build an ark seemed preposterous, he trusted and obeyed God. Not only did he save himself and his immediate family, but the generation of the world was preserved on account of his obedience and trust in God.

Abraham reaped a sure and bountiful reward when he trusted God and packed up all his possessions and sojourned to a strange Land. God blessed him and gave him a promise of a nation that would be great and copious as the sand on the sea. Through Him all nations have indeed been blessed through the promised seed: Jesus.

Moses trusted God and obeyed Him in the face of probable prosecution. He went back to face the demons in his past and to warn Pharaoh. Not only was He spared but He was given the tremendous and prestigious task of being the champion of leading the children of Israel out of bondage and being the arbitrator between God and them.

Joseph trusted and obeyed God, even after he was sold into slavery and forced to live among heathens. He didn't give up his trust despite being accused and thrown in prison. His reward was most remarkable as He was elevated from being an inmate to a distinguished Great.

David trusted and obeyed God so much that God favored and ordained him to be King of Israel. Despite the many attempts to take his life, Saul had no power or authority to harm David as He was protected by the hand of the Almighty who had a special purpose for his life.

There are countless other Bible stars I could speak of who God favored and delivered because they trusted and obeyed. He has never failed on His promises and assurances.

> *The Lord redeemeth the soul of his servants: and none of them that trust in him shall be desolate. (Psalm 34:22).*

Today I want to challenge you: No matter how you are lead to feel odd or different, criticized, ostracized or attacked, inadequate, incompetent and unworthy, sad, broken or rejected, burdened with guilt, shame or stagnation, tired, drained, empty or hopeless, like you have to wait, suffer long and constantly desire more, the key to it all is to: "Trust and Obey for there is no other way, to be happy in Jesus but to trust and obey."

Proclaim proudly that: *"The Lord is my strength and my shield; my heart trusted in him, and I am helped: therefore my heart greatly rejoiceth; and with my heart will I praise him." (Psalm 28:7).*

Eagle Instinct: The eagle's first flight away from its nest is called fledging. As mentioned in an earlier chapter, the parents prepare them for flight by making the nest uncomfortable. They would jump in and out, practicing their balancing as they grow stronger and stronger every day. Whenever the parents observe that their eaglet has developed enough strength in its wings, they place the food on a branch to get the eagles to fly up and get it in order to strengthen their wings. The parents are always watching to catch them if they fall as they eagerly model their parents.

In the same manner, the Lord desires you to trust and obey and model His principles and commands. It is His desire for us to trust that He will not let us fall and, if we do, He will always catch us. If we trust and obey His will, He will guide us through and cause us to mount up and soar in the great life He desires for us.

Prayer:

O Lord, my God, in Thee do I put my trust: save me from all that persecute me and deliver me. You have kept and preserved me from I was in my mother's womb. You have ordered and directed my life up to this point and I know that if I give You my all, if I do Your will consistently and give all praises and glory to You, that You will establish and give me the desires of my heart. Preserve me and cause me to trust and obey You in all things and at all times. Amen.

Chapter 7

To Feel Tired, Drained, Empty And Hopeless

Life is like a kaleidoscopic wheel. It has varied colors and shades. Every now and again we experience the bright, vibrant blushes of happiness, the exciting hues of joy, the light tones of peace and, at other times, the dark tints of sorrow and the strained tinges of emptiness and exhaustion that creeps in.

After exerting ourselves and expending our energies on life, in general, there comes a time when we just feel like rolling over and giving up. However, these moments call for us to rest, reset, replenish and reactivate.

Nia was tired of trying to impress and convince her siblings that she was worthy of their attention and affection. We know this because she just resigned to staying in a corner by herself and watch life go by. We saw the many attacks she suffered and how burdened she became that she resigned to keeping her place and getting out of everybody's way.

When the cares of life press us to a pulp, it is our human nature to give in to the vacuum of exhaustion. Sometimes we get some sort of physical rest or a fleeting moment of peace. But on a whole, some persons never truly experience the truest form of rest.

I want to encourage you to:

1. Rest in His love.
2. Reset in His presence.
3. Replenish and reactivate in His power.

Day 19

Rest In His LOVE

Affirmation

I rest in the love of God, knowing that when the cares of this world press and suppress, I can find peace and immeasurable joy in His Rest.

These things I have spoken unto you, that in me ye might have peace. (John 16:33a).

Two of the most beautiful and magnificent gifts God has given us are His rest and His love. God's rest is synonymous to peace, quiet, tranquility, serenity, stability and calm. His love is deep, profound and all encompassing. When we encounter God's rest, we become familiar with celestial ambiance. When we experience God's agape love, we enjoy the purest, most noble and infinitely fulfilling state of being imaginable. When we get to experience both, we come to know the divinely delightful feeling of being transported to the heavenly realms.

You may ask, is that even possible while we are here in this sinful world? The evidence lies in *1 John 4:16-18:*

And we have known and believed the love that God hath to us. God is love; and he that dwelleth in love dwelleth in God, and God in him. Herein is our love made perfect, that we may have boldness in the day of judgment: because as he is, so are we in this world. There is no fear in love; but perfect love casteth out fear: because fear hath torment. He that feareth is not made perfect in love.

This passage is telling us that when we have the love of God within us, we shall know no fear because perfect love casts out fear and replaces it with boldness. We are assured that no matter what this life serves us, we have security in the love of God.

Therefore, even in the face of death and persecution, we will experience peace and tranquility just like Stephen. Stephen knew what it was to rest in God's love:

And Stephen, full of faith and power, did great wonders and miracles among the people. (Acts 6:8).

And they were not able to resist the wisdom and the spirit by which he spake. (Acts 6:10).

When Stephen was accosted by the suborned men who stirred up the elders, scribes and the people against him, he knew that he was about to meet his demise on account of his faith. However, he was astonishingly calm and peaceful, and the light of God shone through Him.

And all that sat in the council, looking stedfastly on him, saw his face as it had been the face of an angel. (Acts 6:15).

Stephen made a brave, bold, beautiful and heartening last speech that was steeped in the love of God. He recited and gave a comprehensive summary of the Bible from Genesis to the coming of the Lord with much pride, power and passion right before he faced execution. He experienced and encountered the rest found in God's love that even at death He was able to breathe words of peace.

And he kneeled down, and cried with a loud voice, Lord, lay not this sin to their charge. And when he had said this, he fell asleep. (Acts 7:60).

Similarly, Job, while suffering from excruciating and agonizing pain and discomfort, was able to declare words borne of a spirit that was rested in God's love:

Though he slay me, yet will I trust in him. (Job 13:15a).

This is what happens when we are fully immersed in God's love. When we have experienced the rest found in His perfect character, it further affords us:

- **Rest from bitterness:** *Follow peace with all men, and holiness, without which no man shall see the lord: Looking diligently lest any man fail of the grace of God; lest any root of bitterness springing up trouble you, and* *thereby many be defiled. (Hebrews 12:14-15).*

- **Rest from anger:** *But now ye also put off all these; anger, wrath, malice, blasphemy, filthy communication out of your mouth. Put on therefore, as the elect of God, holy and beloved, bowels of mercies, kindness, humbleness of mind, meekness, longsuffering. (Colossians 3:8 &12).*

- **Rest from malice and strife:** *Forbearing one another, and forgiving one another, if any man have a quarrel against any: even as Christ forgave you, so also do ye. And above all these things put on charity, which is the bond of perfectness. And let the peace of God rule in your hearts, to the which also ye are called in one body; and be ye thankful. (Colossians 3:13-15).*

- **Rest from doubt and unbelief:** *Let us labour therefore to enter into that rest, lest any man fall after the same example of unbelief. (Hebrews 4:11).*

For verily I say unto you, that whosoever shall say unto this mountain, Be thou removed, and be thou cast into the sea; and shall not doubt in his heart, but shall believe that those things which he saith shall come to pass; he shall have whatsoever he saith. (Mark 11:23).

- **Rest from fear:** *Abide thou with me, fear not: for he that seeketh my life seeketh thy life: but with me thou shalt be in safeguard. (1 Samuel 22:23).*

  Only fear the Lord, and serve him in truth with all your heart: for consider how great things he hath done for you. (1 Samuel 12:24).

It is in God's love we experience perfect rest. The love God has for us is faultless and incomparable. It is love that prompted Him to create us and it is a greater love that prompted Him to redeem us from our hopeless state when He died for us.

> *But God commendeth His love towards us, in that, while we were yet sinners, Christ died for us. (Romans 5:8)*

He invites us to bask in His love and to find rest therein. We have all experienced burnout at some point in our lives. It is natural for our feeble and frail human nature to suffer exhaustion and to feel drained after exerting energy or doing the same things repeatedly. We get tired, drained and feel depleted when we are constantly under attacks and distress, but more so when we fail to rest in His love. Therefore, when the cares of life press and compress, when trials and burdens distress, we need to rest in His love so He can restore and replenish us.

I encourage you today:

> *The Lord thy God in the midst of thee is mighty; he will save, he will rejoice over thee with joy; he will rest in his love, he will joy over thee in singing. (Zephaniah 3:17).*

Eagle Instinct: Part 1. An extravagant story is told and circulated about the eagle living for seventy years and taking a midlife hiatus to rip out its old feathers and to beat and break its talon and beak on a rock to have them restored in 150 days. I was extremely fascinated by this story as it spoke about going through excruciating pain as a prerequisite for complete restoration and renewal. My intrigue led me to do an extensive research only to discover that it was nothing but a fable. I mourned the trouncing of such a melodramatic story that seemed to carry a sensational message.

I went back and did some contemplation on the true story. The truth is that the eagle has a lifespan of 30 years. It changes its feathers annually or once per year through a process called molting where the old feathers shed naturally, and new ones grow and take their place. Their flight feathers (wing and tail) also falls out one at a time and are replaced in the same manner. There is no pain and grief as it is a natural, unruffled, painless renewal process.

After getting over the initial disappointment of having to disregard the intriguing story that I read first, it came to me that this is how evil intrigues and good appears boring.

However, after prayerful consideration, the Holy Spirit revealed that His work is constant and gradual and is meant to be painless. The Holy Spirit is a Comforter, not a narcissist.

The eagle rests in God's love and He takes care of it as He does the sparrow and preserves it throughout its lifetime. We need not go on a once in a lifetime hiatus to find rest and renewal in pain and horror. Rest and restoration is a daily process and it is meant to be soothing, rather than painful. Hence, like the eagle, we can rest assured that God's protection and care is sustained throughout our lives. Once we remain in Him, He will preserve us as we bask in His rest.

Prayer:

Holy God, I long to rest in Your perfect love. I long to know the peace that passes all understanding. I come to You knowing that You are the true source of love and light. I submit my will to You and ask that You may rock my soul in Your bosom of love. Permeate my life and surround me with Your perfect love as every feeling of emptiness, exhaustion and hopelessness evaporates. Bless and keep me as I learn to extend this love to my fellow men and my sisters in Christ. Bless and hold me up in Your goings. Amen.

Day 20

Reset In His Presence

Affirmation

I bask in the presence of God, knowing that in His presence there is infinite grace and power where I can reset and find restoration.

Thou wilt show me the path of life: in thy presence is fullness of joy; at thy right hand there are pleasures for evermore. (Psalms 16:11).

Moses, the father of meekness, was called and chosen from birth by God. He survived one of history's most extreme mass infanticide. He, by virtue of his gender, was to be annihilated with the possible hundreds, if not thousands, of other male infants who were birthed in his generation from the Hebrew's ethnic group, but God ---

All things certainly worked for good in his situation as he was saved from the ill-fate of being a statistic in the infant mortality record and he was also socially elevated and raised in the care and custody of the Monarch of Egypt. Moses was exposed to the highest levels of comfort and luxury and received the loftiest of upbringing and care; pretty much a fairy tale kind of plot.

However, this fairy tale came to a striking halt when the hour came for him to fulfill his life's purpose. The adored Egyptian heir was to be the redeeming agent for the enslaved Israelites.

Although God orchestrated the events for Moses to be nurtured by the Egyptians, his opulence and affluence were not suitable qualifications for the work God had in mind for him ultimately. In fact, they were more of disincentives rather than advantages. Thus, Moses had to reset in the presence of God by enduring a process of stripping, remodeling, reshaping, de-educating and re-educating, shifting, modifying and altering for him to prove himself worthy and capable of his calling and purpose.

The adored Egyptian heir had to face criticism, rejection, separation, banishment, exile, loneliness, emptiness, exhaustion, months of journeying on foot through a treacherous desert, poverty, simplicity, mentorship from a country stalwart, marriage to a plain country maiden and a shepherd gig. This was the mode of operation and machinery God used to mold, fashion and equip Moses for the holy purpose for which he was called. He was then initiated and consecrated by the omnipotent One Himself through a fiery encounter.

And the angel of the Lord appeared unto him in a flame of fire out of the midst of a bush: and, behold, the bush burned with fire, and the bush was not consumed. (Exodus 3:2).

So it is that when we are ready to be used by God, we must be stripped, reconfigured, reshaped and reset in His presence through treacherous and fiery encounters. God has to burn off the dross so we can be faultless. We have to be empty so He can fill us, and we have to be tired so He can restore us.

Sometimes the people around who support and cheer us on are not the best associates to facilitate the elevation God plans for us. Having everyone's support feels great but doesn't help if they are supporting us for the wrong reasons. Moses was popular in Egypt, but his fans were oppressive and corrupt evil people. He had to be abandoned and rejected by them so that He could make proper associations.

If you find yourself being abandoned, feeling empty, drained and lonely, you may just be in reset mode. The Lord is chastening and fitting you for holy use. He chastens those He loves and is calling you for a holy and higher purpose. Like Brother Jonah, we may not have the privilege to run or hide.

Whither shall I go from thy spirit? Or whither shall I flee from thy presence? (Psalm139:7).

Feeling drained, tired, empty and hopeless is for us to realize that we must depend completely on Him to fill us up.

For in him we live, and move and have our being...For we are also his offspring. (See Acts 17:28).

If you could just see what is playing behind the scenes or what He has in store, you would rejoice. You would bask in His presence and embrace the process of resetting, recognizing that, "*...unto him that is able to keep you from falling, and to present you faultless before the presence of his glory with exceeding joy, to the only wise God our Saviour, be glory and majesty, dominion and power, both now and ever. Amen. (Jude 1:24).*

I, therefore, encourage you to humbly yield. Seek and acknowledge His presence and be mindful that we have to reset in His presence to be worthy to perform the holy and high calling He has on our life.

For thus saith the high and lofty One that inhabiteth eternity, whose name is Holy; I dwell in the high and holy place, with him also that is of a contrite and humble spirit, to revive the spirit of the humble, and to revive the heart of the contrite ones. (Isaiah 57:15).

Eagle Instinct: Part 2. Resetting in God's presence, like every other interaction with the Savior, is restorative. To continue with the story I shared in the previous Eagle

Instinct, if the eagle was to have her feathers plucked out all at once, she would be susceptible to infection. Jerking out the eagle's feathers would cause permanent damage to the feather follicles and would obstruct the possibility of re-growth. Additionally, without feathers the eagle cannot fly. Hence, they cannot hunt for food or escape predators. She would have no defense or security. Also, if her beak or talon was to be knocked off, she would die from the excessive bleeding, infection or starvation.

Like the eagle, we need daily and consistent replenishment and restoration in God's love, presence and power; not a dramatic once in a lifetime hiatus. When God moves to reset us, it brings about complete healing and restoration, not the reverse. He desires for us to have healthy, strong wings to fly; strong functioning beak and talons to feed on His words and share with others. Therefore, like the eagle, we must seek to reset in the Lord's presence daily.

The eagle cleans her beak on the branches, and this keeps it sharp. You need to read the Word of the Lord daily to be kept sharp. In the same way an eagle's feathers shed and are replaced subtly and gradually, it is necessary to refresh yourself regularly through prayer and supplication and retreating at least once per year to be still with God with no form of distraction; just you and God, remembering that in His presence there is fullness of joy.

Prayer:

Great King of kings and Lord of lords, I fall at Your feet, humbly asking You to reset and reconfigure my life. The current setting is corrupted by human associations and selfish pride. Viruses of emptiness, loneliness, exhaustion and hopelessness have crashed the hard drive. I desire for You to activate Your holy software that will remove every filth and blockage that prevent me from fully activating righteous mode. Cleanse and purify my soul as I yield to Your infilling and accept Your grace. Keep me pure and true as I live for You. Amen.

Day 21

Replenish In His Power

Affirmation

I replenish and reactivate in the infinite power of the omnipotent One, knowing that in Him we live and breathe and move.

God is my strength and power: and he maketh my way perfect. (2 Samuel 22:33).

Scientist tells us that:

- About 300 million cells die and are replaced every minute in our bodies.

- The brain processes 600 million bits of visual information per minute.

- A healthy human brain has about 200 billion neurons, each sending as many as 1000 nerve impulses every second.

- The average person has between 100,000 to 150,000 hairs on their head.

- We spend about 10 percent of our waking hours with our eyes closed as we blink 15-20 times every 60 seconds.

- 11ml of oxygen is pumped into our lungs every minute.

- The salivary glands in our mouths produce 1-2 liters of saliva every day.

These are just a few of the amazing facts about the exquisite work of our awe-inspiring God in our bodies; the crowning work of His creation.

How often do we truly contemplate the power of the Almighty? How often do we reflect on His awesome grandeur? Do we have a full grasp of His all-powerfulness, His supremacy over not just the world, but the universe and the heavenly sphere?

We doubt, we languish, and we fear. We also live below our potentials as we give in to afflictions. We court feelings of hopelessness and despondence and we wallow in sorrow and self-pity. Jesus admonishes, *"Ye do err, not knowing the scriptures, nor the power of God. (Matthew 22:29b).*

The God who we serve, *"...telleth the number of the stars; he calleth them all by their names. Great is our Lord, and of great power: his understanding is infinite." (Psalm 147:4-5).*

Job, poetically, attempts to give us a stimulus for us to consider the greatness of our Creator:

He spreads out the northern skies over empty space;
He suspends the earth over nothing.
He wraps up the waters in his clouds;
yet the clouds do not burst under their weight.
He covers the face of the full moon,
spreading his clouds over it,
He marks out the horizon on the face of the waters
For a boundary between light and darkness.
The pillars of heavens quake,
Aghast at his rebuke.
By his power he churned up the sea;
By his breath the skies became fair;
His hand pierced the gliding serpent.
And these are but the outer fringe of his works;
How faint the whisper we hear of Him!
Who then can understand the thunder of his power?"
Job 26:7-14 (NIV)

Such a beautifully picturesque description. Yet, as Job expressed (in different words), this is just a scratch of the surface. How imperative then that we come to realize that as heirs to His throne, we are engrafted and invited through our calling to partake in His magnificence.

According as his divine power hath given unto us all things that pertain unto life and godliness, through the knowledge of him that hath called us to glory and virtue. (2 Peter 1:3).

We don't need to pine away and entertain feelings of hopelessness when we recognize that the all-powerful God who we serve can and will replenish us. There is nothing impossible or unattainable with Him. Remember:

He hath made the earth by his power, he hath established the world by his wisdom, and hath stretched out the heavens by his discretion. When he uttereth his voice, there is a multitude of waters in the heavens, and he causeth the vapors to ascend from the ends of the earth; he maketh lightnings with rain, and bringeth forth the wind out of his treasures. (Jeremiah 10:12-13).

The question is, how do we doubt for a second His ability and power to replenish us when we are drained, empty, exhausted or feel hopeless? Are we aware of how desperately God desires to work in our lives? At this point, our praise pulse should be in high gear. Shout a hallelujah!

Now unto him that is able to do exceeding abundantly above all that we ask or think, according to the power that worketh in us. (Ephesians 3:20).

We need to let go of the stubborn hold we have on the steering of our lives, and give Him the dominion to have

137

His perfect way in us, knowing that He is all-powerful and He has all the solutions to whatever predicament or crisis we may encounter.

> *Let every soul be subject unto higher powers. For there is no power but of God: the powers that be are ordained of God. (Romans 13:1).*

We cannot see with our human eyes, neither can our finite minds grasp the full power of the great I Am! However, He has given us much proof and tangible evidence to convince us that there is absolutely nothing beyond His ability and power to achieve.

> *For the invisible things of him from the creation of the world are clearly seen, being understood by the things that are made, even his eternal power and Godhead; so that they are without excuse. (Romans 1:20).*

I, therefore, challenge you today to yield. Believe that He who created you has the power to replenish and restore you, to fill you with His everlasting joy and grant you the peace that passes all understanding.

> *Now the God of hope fill you with all joy and peace in believing, that ye may abound in hope, through the power of the Holy Ghost. (Romans 15:13).*

Eagle Instinct: Part 3. The story of the eagle's midlife hiatus was told to inspire change. The morale was that in order to survive life, we must initiate a process of change, which may include shedding old friends, habits, beliefs, memories or traditions. Change is deemed necessary to shed the baggage of the past in order to enjoy the present.

While the message was strong and potent, it is not necessary to make up a story about the magnificent eagle to inspire. The eagle has enough intrigue and compelling qualities to inspire. She is replenished daily as she doesn't hold on to old habits, beliefs, bad company or traditions. When we operate in God's presence, love and power, our renewal and replenishment is consistent and sustainable. Like a clock, we are in constant motion.

The eagle is one of the greatest symbol or representation of power highlighted in the Bible. Isaiah 40:31 is the apex for such a theory. Replenishing in God's presence requires us to wait and depend on Him to renew our strength. He promises that we will mount up with wings. The phrase "mount up" is a translation of the Hebrew word *alah,* which means, "ascend, to go up over a boundary." Therefore, God will renew our strength and give us courage to overcome our struggles and the obstacles in our path. We just need to depend on Him and trust His supreme timing.

Prayer:

Mighty God, who in the entire world can truly grasp and comprehend Your nature? Who can truly know the full velocity of Your power? No human instrument can measure Your awesomeness. I, therefore, ask You to forgive me of the times that I doubted You. Pardon me for the moments that I question whether or not You can take me through. Please help me to acknowledge Your replenishing power as You restore me to Your perfection. Please help me to depend on You and to allow You to have Your way. Amen!

Epilogue

Nia felt the wind under her wings for the thousandth time. How she lived without flying for so many years is a marvel she would never fully comprehend. As she glides over the mountains and view the splendid landscape of a 100-mile radius, she reflects and wonders how she survived the confines of a coop and a barn for such a long time. The life she came to embrace and accept as her rightful place and PURPOSE was not achieved overnight or as easily as she would have liked, but the process was well worth it.

It took her awhile to grasp and fully come to terms with **ACTIVATING HER EAGLE INSTINCTS**. It took a lot of patience, dedication and commitment from her savior, Ren, to help and direct her as she morphed into the magnificent eagle she had come to be. Some of the adjustments were mechanical and required no effort as the new environment and associations incited a subtle change process, while others came with painful modification and agonizing sacrifices. But the loving care, compassion, empathy and kindness with which he handled and ushered her conversion from a chicken to an eagle was phenomenal.

She now cherishes her superb vision as an indispensable benefit. Being able to view objects miles away allows her to be more goal-focused and purpose-oriented. She is now able to attack and conquer any prey as she fiercely pursues her targets, making her an extraordinary provider and protector of and for her family.

As a mother, wife and friend to a flock of strong, fierce, resolute, astute eagle ensemble, she is a force to reckon with. She is now fully inducted in the eagle community and operates at an astronomical level. It is such a relief to finally be around creatures of like mind, ambition, attitude and aptitude who challenges her to be a better version of herself daily.

She has come to appreciate what it means to "be still," and has learnt to value moments of reflection and meditation. She learnt how to initiate and test the strength and loyalty of others. She now embraces a life of poise and confidence. She is self-assured and possesses a level of discipline unmatched.

Her love, devotion and appreciation for Ren is awe-inspiring. She regards him with respect, adoration and adulation. Her appreciation and the gratitude she has for him rescuing and transforming her the way he did makes her feel indebted and highly reverential towards him. She sings constant praises to him and basks in daily communion, fellowship and intimacy with him.

She flies regally through each storm that comes her way as she allows the winds to elevate her, rather than intimidate and destroy her. She fights her battles outside of her enemies' comfort zone and takes full control of her life. She trusts her savior for advice and direction and takes counsel as he leads her to higher heights with every lesson he gives.

She has made her nest in a safe territory, away from the reach and interference of intruders and trespassers. She cares for her eggs and her hatchlings with incredible diligence and impeccable care, depending on Ren to assist her in protecting and nurturing them.

She has recently gone on her midlife hiatus and spent time in shedding, replenishing, resetting and renewing her beak, feathers and wings. She has watched her eaglets grow, find their wings and take flight.

Like Nia, it is time to feel the wind beneath your wings. It is full time you enjoyed your wings as you glide through life's challenges and soar into your freedom. Bask in your accomplishments as you overcome all the obstacles you have surmounted and the strength you have garnered in the process.

Over the last 21 days, you have been **ACTIVATING YOUR EAGLE INSTINCTS** and have grown closer to your Lord and Savior who has rescued you; who has descended into the barn of your life and helped you to find your wings and mount up as eagles. He has shown you how to glide through the storms of life, how to overcome and conquer your enemies and many other incredible values and principles to keep you elevated.

Your vision has been sharpened and it is time to navigate your way through life by setting goals and targets and living a PURPOSEFUL existence.

You have learnt to surround yourself with people of like mind who are pursuing righteousness and holiness; who can hold you accountable and sharpen you along your journey.

You have learnt to "be still" and allow your Savior to have His perfect way in your life as you spend quality time meditating, reflecting, contemplating His Words and basking in His presence through incessant prayer and supplication.

You have come to give adoration and adulation to your Lord and Savior; to praise and give Him thanks though the good and bad times and to appreciate that "all things work together for good."

You have learnt to protect your nest and your eggs from possible attacks and from intruders. You have also learnt to take a break from life; to spend time and renew, rest, replenish, restock, restore and re-energize, even though the process is a painful one.

You have learnt to protect and nourish all those in your care and protection and to pass on sound values to your children.

You have learnt to SOAR and mount up with wings! *As an eagle stirreth up her nest, fluttereth over her young, spreadeth abroad her wings, taketh them, beareth them on her wings: So the Lord alone...lead... (See Deuteronomy 32:11-12).*

As Nia perches on a mountain ridge, looking miles below at a place she has come to reflect on as a historical site, she extends her focus and vision as she watches the scene that she once knew as her life. A mother hen trots around with her little yellow fuzzy chicks. She watches pensively as they pick and peck.

She takes it all in as she watches in amazement as a brown overgrown chi-what swoosh pass her mother and siblings at an unnatural speed. She watches in disbelief as she recognizes the color, shape and speed; a sight all too familiar to her. *Another one,* she thought. She instinctively considers rushing to her rescue, but she mechanically remembers a few words Ren shared with her:

> *But they that wait upon the Lord shall renew their strength; they shall mount up with wings as eagles;*

they shall run, and not be weary; and they shall walk, and not faint. (Isaiah 40:31).

That little one, like her, will need to learn at the right time how to **ACTIVATE HER EAGLE INSTINCTS**.

Made in the USA
Columbia, SC
06 March 2020

88731835R00080